A Year on the Wild Side

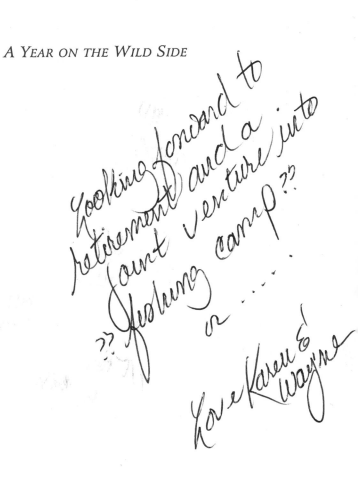

fire-resistant bark
on old trees

cambium layer where bark
and sapwood are laid down annually

springwood 'the wide, light part of ring
summerwood 'the thin, dark part
wind shake or disease healed
with sap.

one
years
growth

DOUGLAS-FIR
Pseudotsuga menziesii

look for mice
under the scales
(bracts)

needles-flat
soft & spirally
arranged.

roots

A YEAR ON THE WILD SIDE

Briony Penn

Horsdal & Schubart

Horsdal & Schubart Publishers Ltd.
Victoria, B.C., Canada

Cover and illustrations by Briony Penn, Saltspring Island, B.C.

This book is set in Bitstream Arrus.

We acknowledge the support of the Canada Council for the Arts for our publishing program. We also wish to acknowledge the financial support of the Government of Canada through the Book Publishing Industry Development Program (BPIDP) for our publishing activities. We also acknowledge the financial support of the Province of British Columbia, through the British Columbia Arts Council.

Printed and bound in Canada by Printcrafters, Inc., Winnipeg, Manitoba.

National Library of Canada Cataloguing in Publication Data

Penn, Briony.
A year on the wild side

Includes bibliographical references and index.
ISBN 0-920663-68-0

1. Natural history—British Columbia—Pacific Coast. 2. Natural history—Washington (State)—Pacific Coast. I. Title.

QH106.2.B7P46 1999   578'.09711'1   C99-910873-5

Printed and bound in Canada

Canadä

Contents

APRIL

DEDICATION

To all the wild ones of the Salish Sea, in particular Donald, Callum and Ronan — my sharpest eyes, fiercest critics and staunchest supporters. And to my father, whose *joie de vivre* is still circling on the thermals.

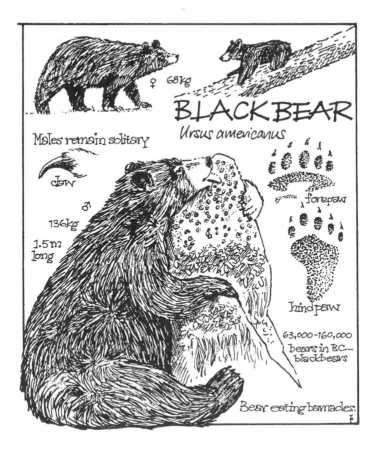

♀ 68kg

BLACK BEAR
Ursus americanus

Males remain solitary

claw

♂ 136kg
1.5m long

forepaw

hind paw

63,000-160,000 bears in BC— blackbears

Bear eating barnacles.

Acknowledgments

E ach of these essays was first published, in a slightly different form, in *Monday Magazine* from 1993 onwards, in a fortnightly column called "Wild Side." Fifty-two of them were selected to create a book that captured a range of natural history events through the calender year. I also tried to represent my better literary efforts. It was hard to make the selection as I have never met two readers who liked the same column best.

I am very grateful to all the staff of *Monday*. I got started thanks to Craig Pipperell, a staff writer, just before the owl called his name. Enormous thanks are due to the three editors: Sid Tafler, who proposed the column; James MacKinnon, who proposed this book; and Ross Crockford, to whom I will propose lunch after this book is published. I also want to thank the three assistant editors, Sherrill Herbert, Shelley Motz and Sharon Hewitt, who shared the twin characteristics of having names beginning with "Sh" and putting up with my poor punctuation cheerfully. To the readers of "Wild Side," I owe you all my thanks for your support and sharing with me your stories. The path to find a publisher was not straight and I am heartily grateful that fate brought Marlyn Horsdal and me together.

In the research and writing of the essays, I have relied heavily upon many people over the years — none of whom are responsible for my mistakes. Thank you so much to my family, especially Rosemary Penn, and to Trudy Chatwin, Ruby Alton, Andy MacKinnon, Syd Cannings, Fenwick Lansdowne, Bristol Foster, Nina Raginsky, Hans Roemer, Fred Salmon, Tim Wahl, Nancy Turner, Dave Fraser, Leah Ramsay, Mairi Gunn, Peggy Frank, Sheila Harrington, Alison Watt, Brian Falconer, Erin Nyhan, Chris Brayshaw, Yorke Edwards, Cris Guppy, Jane Watson, Stan Orchard, Dave Nagorsen, Bruce Whittington, Adolf Ceska, Josi and Olivia Fletcher, Don Gayton, Joyce Lee, Katie Stewart, Jacquie Booth, Ted Davis, Bob Duncan, Rob Butler, Cam Finlay, Kerry Finley, Andrew Bryant, Ian and Karen McAllister, Laura Darling, Alexandra Morton, Adrienne Mason, David Denning, Richard Mackie, Hilary Stewart, Ron Hamilton, Bill Turner, Rick Worrell, Jean Brouard, Terry Frest, Jenny Balke and Tom Wright. To those I forgot, and to my brothers, I apologize.

Note: I have mostly used common names of species. This always poses a problem. Where there might be ambiguity I follow up with the Latin. There are various different protocols for the correct usage, depending on the group of organisms. For consistency, I have capitalized all the common names. This is because a black bear (a bear that is black) is different from a Black Bear.

In some instances, there are discrepancies between the drawings and the text. Nearly a decade has elapsed since some of the articles and drawings were done. The text has been corrected and brought up to date but the drawings have been left in their original form.

One percent of the royalties of this book are going to habitat acquisition through The Land Conservancy of British Columbia (TLC), 5793 Old West Saanich Road, Victoria, BC, V8X 3X3, (250) 361-7693.

Introduction

This book really began in a ditch at midnight. The ditch was near a grove of rare, ancient Garry Oak trees, inhabited by Northern Alligator Lizards, that I had grown up defending. I was in the ditch because I was trying to hide — a challenge, as I was nine months pregnant. Remaining incognito was essential, since I was about to amend one of those Rezoning signs that was hammered into an oak in a cavalier fashion. I stumbled out of the ditch, lumbered to the sign and painted "REZONE FOR OAKS" in red under cover of darkness, then fell back into the ditch. Panting there, I pondered if there wasn't an easier way to whip up enthusiasm for a disappearing natural world.

Almost nine years, two boys and nearly 200 columns later, I still haven't made up my mind which is easier — writing on signs or writing in newspapers. There is a certain amount of risk in both and I still work at midnight, sometimes in ditches. I also haven't made up my mind which is more successful from the point of view of the lizards and the oaks. What occurred to me most vividly, that night in the ditch, was that the environmental movement is rich in humour and paradox. There is something absurd, but poignant, about composing slogans for a bunch of lizards that would rather meet a slug in a ditch than a pregnant woman well past her bedtime. Our paradoxical attitudes to the natural world have been as much a source of wonderment to me as the species that inhabit it. So the book is a social and natural history comedy, written in metaphorical red paint, about this place.

"This place" is the shores of the "Salish Sea" nestled in the heart of "Wrangellia" — both manufactured place names. I heard a Salish woman in the San Juan Islands use the name Salish Sea and I borrowed it. The linguistic boundaries of the Salish people evolved within the distinctive inland sea that empties into the Pacific. It stretches from the Straits of Georgia and Juan de Fuca down to Puget Sound. The two regional newspapers that I write for serve the central shores of the Salish Sea — Victoria's *Monday Magazine* and the *Gulf Islands Driftwood*, and there is no other English name for this inland sea. No name for one of the ecologically richest inland seas in the world? It was like writing about the Mediterranean without having a name for it.

As for Wrangellia, I borrowed that name from a bunch of wild geologists. They theorize that the west coast islands were once collectively a super-island called Wrangellia somewhere in the South Pacific that drifted and eventually crashed into North America. It is a compelling argument and helps explain lots of things, like why west coasters form a distinctive culture and stop for tea in the afternoon. Wrangellia is the subject of my second essay and the name of my gumboot dancing group.

The arrangement of this book is as 52 weekly essays collected under the months of the year — an almanac-esque form. Turn to the first week in August and you'll find out what berries to pick that week. Another week will be why the termites are swarming, or where the herring are spawning or when the maple leaves are falling. Embedded in the natural history chat will be tips on how to increase your berry patch or save the herring. There is also the odd philosophical meditation on subjects such as why we have pest exterminators or what is the future of our maple leaf flag. The coast is a busy place, especially in the winter, and there is something every week to evoke enthusiasm, once you get to know it.

For each column, I did an illustration. Some people only look at the pictures and that is fine. When I see my drawings pinned up in school classrooms I feel quite gratified. As a school kid in Victoria, I was subjected to endless pictures of Cardinals, Blue Jays and Bison shipped out by textbook imperialists from the east. Every nature book had a Kangaroo and Gila Monster but where was a picture of our local Roughskin Newt? It's no accident that we haven't valued our indigenous community. Anyone is welcome to use these pictures in their classrooms or for non-profit use. The drawings are in black and white so they can be photocopied, enlarged and coloured — an alternative to Mickey Mouse.

The first and only journalism trick I learned at the newspaper was the device of a hook to lure in your readers. I will use any devious means to get a hook: e.g., start off columns with sex or rock stars. This all stems from my feeling that most people think nature writers are sexless, earnest sorts of people. And that nature writing doesn't relate to their lives, though really it is the crazy comedy that surrounds them.

Which takes me back to the ditch and why I got started in this business in the first place. Where that grove of oak trees was is now a church and a huge parking lot. I dream that one day that congregation will suddenly have a change of heart and want to restore their land back to the grove of oak trees. Who knows, they might see the light in the eyes of the alligator lizards. So when I write I'm always thinking of that congregation.

I also write for a woman in red spandex whom I met in a nightclub. I was there doing a variety show in aid of another grove of doomed Garry Oaks — a little bit of preaching, a little bit of singing and a little bit of Wrangellian gumboot dancing. After too much of the first she yelled at me, "Just shut up and keep dancing." For the red spandex lady and others like her, here is my gumboot dance beside the glitterball of the Salish Sea.

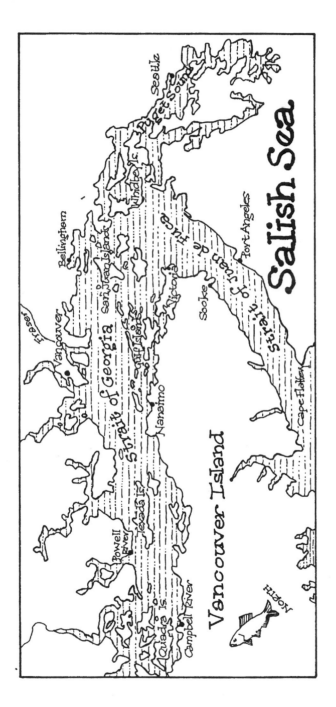

January

ANOTHER SEASIDE ATTRACTION

She was washed up on the shore — a quiet mass of mottled pink flesh diminishing, even in the thin heat of the January sun. The remaining arms and glassy eyes were the only recognizable features that identified her. We stared at her, along with the crows hopping anxiously at a safe distance from us. She was a Giant Pacific Octopus (*Octopus dofleini*). Her arms would have curled from my head to my toes had we met each other deep in Saanich Inlet on the east coast of Vancouver Island, where she washed in from. Grounded, she stretched four metres (12 feet) from tip to tip. She became a seaside attraction; everyone came to look at her until another high tide dragged her back into the sea, slightly the worse for wear. I checked her every day out of a sense of duty — an irrational kinship with this mound of evaporating flesh, anxious to see her well thought of by the visitors.

Most people who have lived on or by the sea have an octopus story and I heard some of them during my vigil by her side. One fisherman told a story about trying to chase an octopus, that had come up in his net, around the decks. The octopus raced ahead, tentacles flying, eventually squeezing its huge body through the gunwales to escape. One old halibut fisherman told me he had a fear of them, a fear shared by many coastal people, even though

1

they were used for bait. Once his deckhand got wrapped up in the tentacles of an octopus he was trying to kill. The captain threw them both into the fishhold so that he wouldn't have to see the deckhand eaten alive. The mate escaped out of the hold, threatened to eat the captain alive and abandoned ship with the live octopus.

One scuba diver recounted a story about a male threatening him when he interrupted a breeding session. The males enlarge and modify part of one of their tentacles into a sexual organ with which they remove a package of sperm a metre long from their mantle and deposit it in the mantle of the female. The arm of a Giant Pacific Octopus is daunting enough at 20 metres below the surface without being twice its normal size, laden with sperm and waving at you. An aquarium buff testified to the fact that octopi have long-term memories, unlike any other invertebrates, and can perform problem-solving tricks.

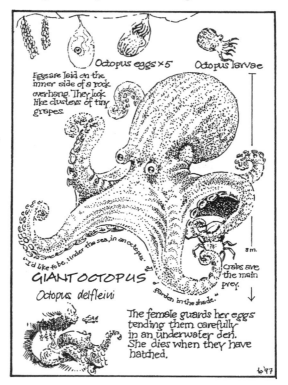

Octopus eggs × 5   Octopus larvae

Eggs are laid on the inner side of a rock overhang. They look like clusters of tiny grapes.

"I'd like to be, under the sea, in an octopus..."

GIANT OCTOPUS
Octopus delfleini

"...garden in the shade."

3 m.

Crabs are the main prey. ↓

The female guards her eggs tending them carefully in an underwater den. She dies when they have hatched.

A marine biologist told me she had seen swarms of young octopi in their larval stage changing colours from brilliant green to deep blue as they swam on the surface of the sea, feeding on the plankton before they sink to the bottom to start their adult life. An eight-year-old boy told me that a Giant Pacific Octopus could eat a BC Ferry. A six year old told me that if you blindfold an octopus it can tell the difference between two objects. These were all pertinent anecdotes, but I needed an octopus expert. Octopus experts are thin on the ground. I needed one to answer a simple question asked me by everyone who visited the roadside attraction: why did she die?

We don't know a great deal about the lives and times of this species but this is what I did discover. They dwell along the shores between Oregon and Alaska, and the largest ones in the world have been discovered in Saanich Inlet, near Victoria on Vancouver Island. Everything loves to eat baby octopi but it's not known if anything preys on the large adults.

The first scientific documentation of the breeding cycle appears to have been done on the coast in 1922 by a Dr. Fisher, whose study on breeding behaviour substantiated the scuba diver's tale. He goes on to note that a couple of months after fertilization, thousands of eggs looking like long bunches of sultana grapes were laid by a female he kept in captivity. She attached them to the ceiling of a den in a tank. The female tended her eggs, swooshing water through her siphon over them, carefully cleaning them with her suction cups and forming her body into a basket shape around them to keep them safe from predators. He never saw her leave them, nor accept food. Instead, she picked up food offered her and, flushing reddish-brown, would hurl it away from her den. The eggs started to hatch into tiny larvae two months later and she stood guard by them until the last egg hatched. She died shortly thereafter. Since then, Dr. Fisher's historical observations have been repeated in the wild many times over. Octopus may live beyond five years, but as soon as they breed, they die, like salmon.

This was the crucial piece of information I was looking for. My intuitive regard for this overworked mother (they can brood up to 200,000 young) was justified. I could empathize with the exhausted heap of mottled pink flesh with only two glassy eyes and a few remaining arms — there are many of us who answer to that description. Hounded by fishermen, chased into tight corners, battling with ferries, performing party tricks behind glass and still finding time to suction off dirty offspring, she deserved to lie in dignity.

WRANGELLIAN REFUGEES FROM THE SOUTH SEA: ONE DAY WE'LL ALL BE GNEISS TO EACH OTHER

One midwinter day I was feeling so bleak I read a geological journal. Between the dust mites, I read about a theory which blew away my blues better than a southeaster. The theory concerns continental drift and the story of "our continent." As it turns out, "our continent" had nothing to do with North America until we had the misfortune to crash into it 100,000,000 years ago. Our continent is Wrangellia and if North America (or Laurentia as geologists called that land mass) hadn't been in the way, the inhabitants of the Pacific Northwest would be Wrangellians, still drifting happily around the Pacific Ocean.

Two hundred and seventy million years ago, the Gulf and San Juan islands, Vancouver Island, Haida Gwaii (the Queen Charlottes) and the islands of Alaska, were one massive island in the making, 10,000 kilometres away in the South Pacific Ocean. This was a pleasurable notion to me because it explained many things — why I hated ice hockey, why I liked to lie under the trees and watch the world go by, why I had a spiritual kinship with other islanders and why I felt compelled to stop for tea or other refreshment at four o'clock — the South Pacific was my spiritual homeland.

Those who study rocks and fossils are responsible for this theory. Don't let the appearance of dusty rocks suggest that geologists lead dull lives. From various chemical and magnetic experiments and the fossil patterns of rocks, geologists construct epic dramas about continents being made, charging across seas and crashing into each other. For example, the rocks under your feet as you read this contain evidence that they were made from volcanoes gaily spewing their lava and ash into the steamy, turbid waters of the South Pacific.

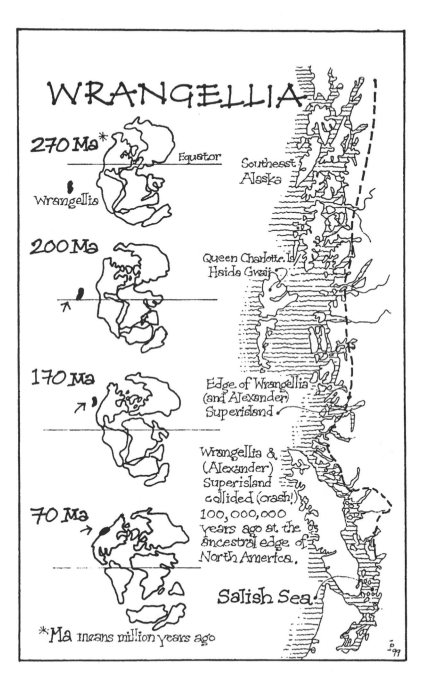

WRANGELLIA

270 Ma*

Equator

Wrangellia

Southeast
Alaska

200 Ma

Queen Charlotte. Is
Haida Gwaii

170 Ma

Edge. of Wrangellia
(and Alexander)
Superisland

70 Ma

Wrangellia &
(Alexander)
Superisland
collided (crash!)
100,000,000
years ago at the
ancestral edge of
North America.

Salish Sea

*Ma means million years ago

As the sea washed around the shores, great swarms of marine creatures with names like *elasmosaurs, mosasaurs, lithophagas* and *crinoids* clung, bred and died upon the rocks, creating over time the limestone beds. Upon the land grew gingko trees, palm trees, pine trees and ancestors of the Garry Oak which fell into swamps and were immortalized in the fossil record. The sea floor spread and Wrangellia was carried northward. New volcanoes spread more lava on top while underneath, the molten rocks solidified into granite. When we hit the western edge of North America (we were one of many super-islands or "terranes" crashing into the edge), the land scrunched up, forming the Coast Mountains.

Apart from the allure of a great action drama, our geological heritage has two bearings on day-to-day life that are comforting. First, Wrangellia reminds us that life is transitory. Much of Wrangellia has already disappeared under the continent of Laurentia. At its most mobile, it moved at almost the same rate as human hair grows. Even at half this rate, most of Wrangellia could disappear over the epochs. Monument-builders and excessive avarice upset me, especially in January, so I find comfort in the fact that the only humans that will be immortalized will be those who throw themselves into a swamp and turn up in the fossil record 100,000,000 years later. Most of our puny efforts to leave a mark will be sucked under a continent and metamorphosed into the thinnest veneer of gneiss.

Once I knew that life was gneiss, I discovered a second reassuring idea. Our distinct heritage has its origins in the South Pacific. To be exact, Wrangellia was formed in the vicinity of the Marquesas archipelago. The Marquesas are where Gauguin lived and painted. Everything there is purple, scarlet and green, life is gentle and wildflowers are still honoured. The human history of the Marquesas is a good example of the changes in people when they settle on the shores of volcanoes formed in the Pacific.

The Polynesians discovered the islands 2,000 years ago, a mere millisecond in geologic time. They arrived with fervour, as all invading things do. Half of the bird species were hunted into extinction before a century was out, and their municipal councillors spent all of their time building monuments, swinging subdivision deals and creating schemes that involved human sacrifice. Not surprisingly, their monumental culture collapsed and the citizens adapted to a more leisurely lifestyle in the forest. For example, today on the island of Tahuata there are no hotels and the ferry is a fishing boat.

So now when I go get my hair trimmed, I remember that all the architectural monuments to Laurentian commerce, including big-box stores and ice hockey arenas, will be that many centimetres closer to getting sucked under the continent and converted into gneiss. And in the meantime, I understand why I long for summer days when I can frolic on these volcanic shores, act like a *crinoid* and stop for an occasional cup of tea.

WHAT RHYMES WITH PIGEON?: WIGEON

There is a certain amount of responsibility in living with wigeon. There is even more of a responsibility in writing about wigeon. Wigeon are very important small ducks that grace the shores of the entire northern hemisphere and they deserve great literature. Having set out to find some examples of the world's literature on the subject, I have found myself in the unenviable position of drawing a blank. This is very surprising, as wigeon rhymes with pigeon and I would have thought that maybe even some secondary poet of the 19th century (when they used the spelling "widgeon" and "pidgeon") might have felt moved to do a rhyming couplet with the two.

The reason I felt instinctively that wigeon should have been afforded some mention in history is that we have been fellow shore-dwelling companions during the winters since the beginning. Wigeon flock to coastal estuaries and mudflats in the winter, then disperse in the spring throughout the continent to breed. The American Wigeon inhabits the Pacific shore and the Eurasian Wigeon inhabits Eurasia. Sometimes Eurasians get blown off course into flocks of Americans and vice versa. (We call it APEC.) Both species are distinctive for their light-coloured pates or foreheads, white wingbars and lovely soft whistle. Whether you are living along the coast of Japan, Spain, Britain,

Newfoundland or here on the Pacific you will have shared your time, maybe unknowingly, with a wigeon.

When I did my literature review, I was looking particularly for any reference to the wigeon and their common names — not just "duck." This may have limited my scope somewhat but I was after a writer who knew, loved and understood the very particularness of the wigeon. Those irridescent green swaths of eyebrows in the American Wigeon drake that give you a glimpse of an emerald world. Or the fabulous red ones of the Eurasian Wigeon that evoke rich tapestries and exotic bazaars. That arched buff belly that rises out of the water when a joyous stretch is prompted by the arrival of a mate. That flash of sunlight in the white feathers of the wingbars as they come in to

land on the sheltered waters of the bay. Those feelings of cama-
raderie in the flock as they push back the tide with their bills to
harvest the rich mudflats below. And finally someone, but
someone, must have recalled the pleasure of the soft, whistled
greetings in the flat, early dusk of the winter solstice.

I had a whole assortment of key words with which to conduct
my search. An old name for wigeon is "baldpate." Not surprisingly this drew a blank; there were no Odes to a Baldpate.
Another old name was "butterball." This is the affectionate
name provided by early settlers who discovered the local prefer-
ence for these fat, tasty little ducks during the long dreary
winters. Now at least we were getting into alliteration and
maybe there would be a tribute by some half-starved, homesick
colonist for the ubiquitous butterball. Alas, I haven't found one.
I found a Cree reference which described the bird by its whistle.
My Coast Salish sources didn't turn up any direct references to
wigeon, which I felt was probably a reflection of the ethnogra-
pher's — not the locals' — ignorance of the distinctions between
the ducks.

Turning to Asia, I thought of my pair of Japanese carved ducks
— a drake and duck — and examined them in detail to see if
they were wigeon. In both China and Japan these ducks are
supposedly part of every married household. The woman uses
them to indicate the state of her amorous feelings for her
husband. If she puts the female facing the male, then the
husband knows he can expect a little loving that night. What an
opportunity for finding some steamy romantic eastern literature,
all hung around the metaphor of the wigeon. However, upon
close examination the ducks were painted to represent the noisy
and far less romantic Mallard.

Of course, my search was not exhaustive; I had a deadline for
writing a column and I still had the original responsibility to
describe how to live well with wigeon. It was a great disappointment to find any number of descriptions of how to live badly
with birds and nothing for how to live well with them. Perhaps
this is the origin of our current world crisis.

I did find one reference to wigeon. It was a corporate commu-
nications strategy handbook that set out the corporate way to

communicate with human beings. A picture of a flock of wigeon was used as an example of good "issue management strategy" by a chemical corporation to tart up its image — which was in danger of losing "external stakeholders" because perceptions of "corporate responsibility" were unfavourable. A bunch of wigeon in their annual reports would obviously convince us that they were now a thoughtful, responsible little lot.

Well, I am back to my original premise. There is a certain amount of responsibility living with wigeon. There is even more of a responsibility in writing about them.

Snowy Owls and Other Temperance Angels

Who comes from the North Pole, only says "ho ho ho" in passionate frustration and leaves nothing at Christmas except pellets? The first clue is that a pellet is the regurgitated remains of a meal. The pellets have a diameter of 27 millimetres (one inch) and a length of 100 millimetres (four inches) — an especially important statistic for those keen on numbers. The second clue is that these pellets can be found in coastal flood plains around the Salish Sea, places like Boundary Bay, during a particularly hard winter. The third clue is that to my knowledge Santa Claus has not been spotted dining out here on the coast and I doubt that he regurgitates — it would pose a problem from an open sleigh stacked full of presents with a reinful of rampant Caribou.

If you have not guessed, here are two more easy clues. This visitor normally has a diet of small, guinea-pig-like creatures that reproduce explosively every three weeks, live for only a year and go on fictitious marches *en masse* over cliffs. (Actually, the population collapses as they outstrip their food supply.)

The second easy clue is that they are snowy white, large and belong to the owl family. You still may not guess, in which case you are forgiven because you might have missed Snowy Owls in their cyclical migrations to the coast. Bumper owl years happen every ten years or so. The cycle occurs when lemming populations crash in the north and the owls range southward and coastward to live off such delicacies as waterfowl and seagulls.

A Snowy Owl pellet is full of feathers, bones beaks & other indigestible bits of prey.

25 mm

100 mm

Occasionally mistaken as angels, but never by the Northern Bog Lemming.

115 cm

Snowy owls only come south during bad winters in the north. Flecking indicates younger owls and females.

SNOWY OWL
Nyctea scandiaca

Tens to hundreds of owls can be spotted hanging out in farmers' fields or near marinas, picking off Buffleheads. These events provide you with a lovely opportunity to view their full 60-to-70-centimetre (20-to-27-inch) bodies up close — smaller but a great deal more interesting to look at than a fat old man in a red suit.

The three most distinctive things about Snowy Owls are that they are diurnal (awake during the day), ground perching and silent. If you travel to the North Pole you will understand why they have developed these characteristics. I spent one week on Victoria Island, just south of the North Pole, wandering the tundra at midsummer. There is no choice about being diurnal; I kept forgetting to go to sleep. As for perching on the ground, there is also no choice. The highest object that I found on which to perch looking for Snowy Owls and Caribou was one of those megapellets with a one-inch diameter. I was probably the highest thing, next to a musk-ox, for hundreds of miles. Snowy Owls feel relatively secure sitting on the ground watching for possible predators. As a result, forest dwellers, used to birds perching in trees, often walk right past them thinking they are half-melted snowmen. As far as silence goes, a Snowy Owl only needs to call attention to itself during the breeding season. I have also found this a useful maxim to live by.

Despite the name, these owls are not entirely white. Most birds have some dark flecking on their foreheads and sides, although very large adult males get very snowy. On the coast, you often get reports of sightings that go something like this: "I was sitting in my kitchen after my twelfth cup of Christmas cheer when this white angel flew by my window."

These sightings become near-religious experiences for people, which fuels them to do great works for the earth, join temperance societies and dedicate their lives to angels, miracles and splendid deeds. After my time on Victoria Island, when I had a near-religious experience with a long-dead shaman woman and a Snowy Owl, I am inclined to think that an angel and a Snowy Owl are one and the same thing, but at the time of writing I haven't yet joined a temperance society.

February

RIVER OTTERS ON THE STEPS: RUNNING WILD WITH CIVIC PRIDE

I got this idea from a German punk rocker that I met in front of the Legislative Buildings in Victoria. We were standing looking out across the harbour over a small bronze sculpture of some River Otters, and we started talking about punk art and nature. She told me that once, in her town of Kassel, an artist was commissioned to create a civic sculpture in front of the town hall. He arrived at the installation ceremony with 7,000 chunks of heavy basalt and dumped them on the steps of the hall. The *burgermeister* had to climb over them to get to the front door. Then the artist announced that the sculpture was called "7,000 Oaks." He would plant an oak for every one of his chunks of rock in public spaces so that eventually, the town hall could have their steps back and the town would have a sculptural legacy of 7,000 oaks. The town found enough places for the oaks.

Naturally, we agreed that "7,000 Oaks" was a stroke of genius. In her country, with a plethora of indestructible sculptures of stout men riding to battle on horses, it was a more-than-welcome

13

relief to those who had seen enough battles for a while. I told her that it was a welcome relief to me to see the River Otters, even frozen in bronze, since I was accustomed to the ilk of Queen Victoria, who ranks somewhere near the stout warriors in historical context. As we talked she got more and more keen to go and see some real live oaks and otters, which weren't apparent in the turmoil of pleasure cruisers, float planes and Legislative landscaping. I sent her up to Beacon Hill Park to see both. I'd heard a young otter had taken up residence at the duck pond. Since otters in Germany have the scarcity value of Blue Whales, she was off like a weasel and I was left at the harbour expanding on variations of "7,000 Oaks."

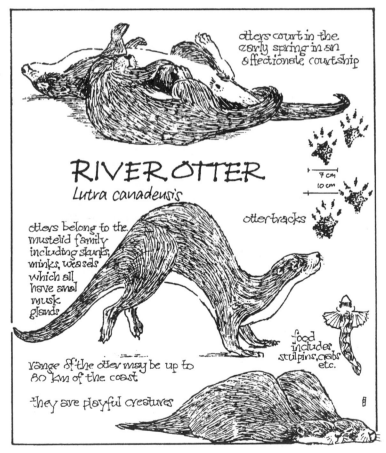

otters court in the early spring in an affectionate courtship

RIVER OTTER
Lutra canadensis

otters belong to the mustelid family including skunks, minks, weasels which all have anal musk glands

otter tracks

7 cm
10 cm

food includes sculpins, crabs etc.

range of the otter may be up to 80 km of the coast

they are playful creatures

Why stop at the oaks? I thought. Think of all the restorative projects that you could initiate for a civic pride project *extraordinaire*. The otters gave me the idea for a second sculpture. Given that thousands of rocks had been deposited by the city fathers in a beautiful wild bay for an ill-advised berm, why not erect a sign on the pile that said "1,000 Otter Homes."

River Otters currently rely on seeking out protected niches, like rock piles, along neglected parts of the coastline and lakeshores to raise their families, which they are doing this month. Finding neglected parts of the coastline, as anyone seeking waterfront property can assure you, is getting harder and harder, and the otters are vulnerable to lots of disturbance — berms, manicured shoreline, cats and dogs. Getting the city fathers to build otter homes by redistributing their rock pile along the coast could be a highly successful form of creating secure otter habitat. It would also keep them from doing more ill-advised projects.

Then I thought I might attach a "50,000 Salamanders" sign to a passing log boom. For every log put back into our forests as a nurse log, we would be creating habitat for five salamanders. Salamanders, like all amphibians, are vanishing because they are vulnerable to industrial forestry. If forest cover is removed and the spongy old logs that they live in dry out, they dry out too. They are one of the most prolific predators of small invertebrates (not to be confused with stout men) and forests need predators of small invertebrates.

We could start by having "20 Salamanders" assigned to the front of the Legislative Buildings. It needs a few nurse logs to break up the tedium of the lawn. Queen Victoria would enjoy their company — a change from some of the political lizards that have crawled through the grounds. I know my friend the punk rocker would have enjoyed seeing them — her hairdo was modelled after the rare European Great-crested Newt.

The problem with this idea is that it is a little too exciting and could be dangerous if it falls into the hands of someone with different objectives. Imagine someone depositing one million chunks of asphalt on the government's steps and calling it "One Highway." We might wake up one day to find that the whole landscape has been lined with chunks of asphalt by some madman in the name of art. Maybe that's already happened.

Horsetails and Alpha Males: Explore the Dinosaur Within

You might have heard a sigh of relief riding above the air currents as February blew in. It was on account of a small event that comes every year about this time almost everywhere in the world — the bursting through of the Common Horsetail bud (*Equisetum arvense*). The significance of this annual event, which has been going on for several hundred million years, is only apparent if you have had the opportunity to spend a long winter enclosed within four walls with small alpha-male-hopefuls who relate only to dinosaurs.

"Alpha male" is the term biologists use to describe the dominant male in a wolf pack. Male cubs, when they are young, vie for the alpha male position. They make themselves thoroughly unpopular during the long winter days and nights cooped up in the den by constantly asserting their dominance over everything from their mother's teats to their sisters' dinners. What alpha males need most is an outlet for their energies and a wolf mother's solution varies little from most humans — relentless outdoor activities with objects that help them channel their energies. Being a '90s parent with two emerging alpha males is challenging, since aggression for catching food and mates isn't necessarily the most helpful of qualities to include on their *résumés* these days. Thank goodness, the natural world has provided an outdoor activity designed exclusively for our alphas; it all centres around the horsetail.

The horsetails or *Equisetum* are a genus of plants that have been growing in wettish gravelly areas forever. Their street credibility for young males is in having been witness to dinosaurs. In fact, the ancestors of the strange, slender, hairy, primeval-looking plants you see today were dinner for dinosaurs. And if you lie down in a horsetail patch, you can look up into the whorls of green branches and vestigial black leaves and almost

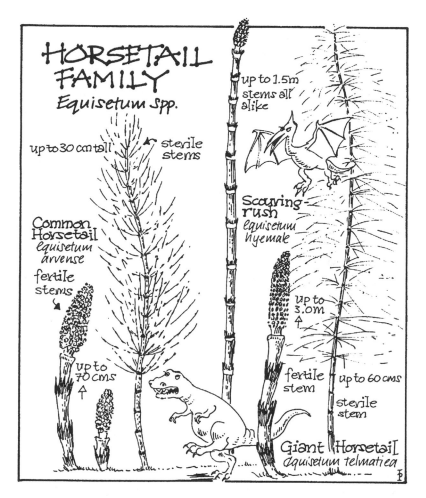

believe that you are a *Diplodocus* munching in the Carboniferous
horsetail forests 370,000,000 years ago, on the watch for the
ever-ferocious *Tyrannosaurus rex* — the embodiment of every
young alpha male's dream.

So that is where you will find this wolf mother with her
cubs as soon as the first fertile stems come pushing their
stalks through the moist spring earth. Horsetails are one of
the first plants in spring to start growing. The Common or
Field Horsetails first send up fertile stems which are pale in
colour and shaped appropriately like spears. Then, closely

17

following come the infertile stems from which their inappropriate name is derived. I have never seen a horse with a tail like these. The beauty of a horsetail patch is that they are one of the most widespread and resilient plants in the world. They survived the dinosaurs and the eruption of Mount Saint Helens, so they can survive my cubs. Would-be dinosaurs can roll in them, snatch them in their carnivorous jaws and break them off and use them as prehensile weapons. Parents can position themselves as slumbering *Brontosaurus* in the horsetail forest and rest assured that if they are attacked from above by the fierce *Pterodactyl* they don't have to worry about the furniture or the stereo being crunched in his gargantuan beak.

As a slumbering *Brontosaurus*, I prefer the species of Giant Horsetail as they are very tall and feathery, and you can almost get a short nap before *T. rex* zeroes in on you. I find the Scouring Rush, which looks like asparagus growing in the ditch, doesn't afford you enough cover and the Swamp Horsetail is rather damp. I can assure you, however, that all of the above break into segments upon impact. So, only minimally battered and bruised we pick ourselves up from the horsetail patch and retire — all passion spent — for a restorative cup of horsetail tea.

GONDOLAS AMONGST THE SKUNK CABBAGE: VENICE OF THE PACIFIC

There are no Skunk Cabbages in Venice. I found this very odd because this is the sort of place I would have expected to find them: big swampy areas that smell of rotting vegetables. The fact that Venice is missing this superb specimen of the Calla Lily family makes our swamps a better choice than Venice for a Mardi Gras holiday. Millions may flock to see a bunch of jaded gondoliers punting around the San Giorgio *basino* but I can witness all by myself the private performance of the Water Boatmen insects, emerging from their winter dormancy. The glitterati might get their thrills wearing masks of Harlequin, but down in the swamp I can see a real Harlequin duck fly over.

I am all in favour of watching Pagliacci sneak off with the Countess into a rotting stone palace, but imagine a Hooded Merganser sneaking off with his masked princess into a decaying tree. The aristocratic Doges of Venice with large noses and furry hats can't shine a light next to our bears with bigger noses and fur all over. Tintoretto's clouds can't compare with swamp mist. Some might desire the romantic winding canals and bridges with those tall lanterns and the Ca d'Oro lighting their way. But nothing can equal the network of canals and lichen-covered wood bridges through which the Skunk Cabbage burst into brilliant yellow bloom — lighting your way for a west coast Mardi Gras in the swamp.

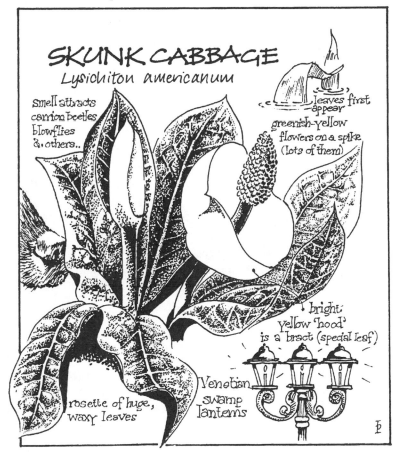

SKUNK CABBAGE
Lysichiton americanum

smell attracts carrion beetles blowflies & others..

leaves first appear

greenish-yellow flowers on a spike (lots of them)

bright yellow 'hood' is a bract (special leaf)

Venetian swamp lanterns

rosette of huge, waxy leaves

Yes, the swamp is the place for me, come the melt of the snow, along with every bear, blowfly and other lovers of smelly objects. This lovely lily shines like the first beacon in a dark, dreary sea of winter. Enthusiasts prefer to give it better press and call it the "swamp lantern" for that reason. It needs no press in the animal world, though. Carrion beetles and blowflies all crawl out like the *paparazzi* in San Marco square with their shiny jackets and embroidered wings in search of the brightest houses of ill repute. Accustomed to laying their eggs on smelly flesh, they are fooled by this plant and help pollinate it.

Black and Grizzly Bears emerge from their winter hibernation and go straight to the succulent new growth of the flower for their first meals. The Skunk Cabbage is so important to their diet that part of the reason we are losing our bears is that we are losing our swamps. Bears alone have the palate for the flesh of this plant. Those who have tried to eat it say it is like eating crushed glass. Even Venetian glass makers haven't come up with a glass that is a brighter, purer yellow than this beacon of the swamp.

So I am off to the swamp this Mardi Gras. I might even catch some good theatre. There is a play on with the same plot as the marionette show in the *teatro* off the Grand Canal. It starts off with the Harlequins, Doges, courtiers and countesses revering their Venice, treasuring their Tintorettos, guarding their gondolas and loving their lanterns. They also spend a great deal of time sneaking off in their gondolas with each other. One day, a spoilsport puppet comes along and threatens to take away all their fun — drain the canals, cast out all the Harlequins and angels, put out all the lanterns and send the Doge with the furry nose to prison. On the way to prison, the Doge has to pass over the Bridge of Sighs where prisoners traditionally got their last glimpse of Venice before descending into an airless, dark cell. So in love with this scene is he that he leaps off the Bridge of Sighs and vows to wreak vengeance on the spoilsport messing everything up. I think he sends Countess Merganser to seduce the spoilsport and in the end everyone lives happily ever after. The bad guy becomes a carefree Water Boatmen — plying his way up and down, singing as he goes between the swamp lanterns.

A WHALE OF A TIME:
A BRUSH OVER THE BOW WITH MARINE MAMMALS

In this blue time of the year of late February, I once decided to go to sea, lie down in a canoe and watch clouds. This was all in aid of trying to approach the year with a calm and unanxious state of mind. I was going to rest my eyes on nothing but grey expanses of fluffy clouds and the odd seagull — objects which, I believe, have no claim of possession upon them and which cannot be developed or logged. The Romans referred to these objects as *communia omnia* which means "property of all" and sounds like a meditative chant (which would be useful for the event). The day was calm, overcast, and mild — perfect for my sojourn. I nestled myself into the canoe, set off on a gently ebbing tide and floated out to sea.

The beauty of bobbing along in a battered canoe lying down is that no one knows you are in there. They just see a piece of old fibreglass, which no one feels compelled to clean up or salvage. I imagine I could float in my battered canoe around the world, down the Ganges, through Bosnia and up the Nile with never an interruption or an altercation. Almost invisible except to the clouds and the odd seagull, I might even achieve nirvana on the Nile. But back to the sea.

This particular day, I was going to just float for a good part of a day, about the length of an ebbing tide, hoping that the moon would then start to pull me and the waters back from whence we came. After one hour, I had exhausted the possibilities of *communia omnia* as both a chant and a concept, at least from that vantage point. I had failed to spot even one Glaucous-winged Seagull, as all the sea birds were either obscured in the mist or bobbing around the canoe waiting for the eagles to finish me off.

I was in the process of reconciling myself to not having what it takes to reach nirvana when I was suddenly deafened by the flapping of wings. Right over my canoe exploded ten herons, every which way. This is quite an experience as their air displacement is equivalent to a jet plane taking off. Crossing my line of vision came a heron tree (large, old Douglas-fir with lots of bare

21

branches) jutting out over the water. I had obviously surprised them off their roost and they were fleeing from the apparition in front of them. I spent the next few minutes imagining their conversation when I floated into view. A singing log? Expectant halibut? Product from the sewage outfall?

I can safely say that the Great Blue Heron is best viewed from below. You get the full appreciation of their long breast feathers which trail like streamers in the breeze. You also get to see their long angular bodies take flight. Their wings extend, their neck

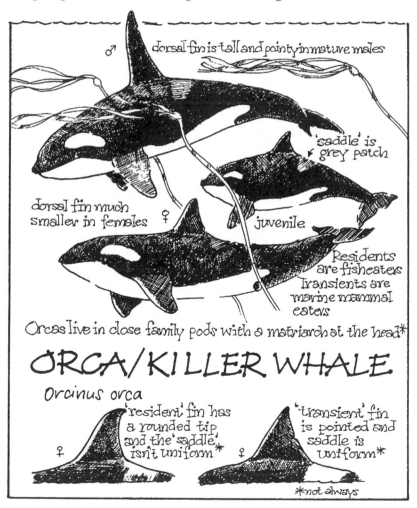

retracts like a telescope and their legs flail around to balance them against updrafts. So happy was I at this break in the tedium of the previous hour that I failed to notice the first signs of the next visitors.

It came to my attention that there was a gentle rocking of the canoe that wasn't present earlier. I assumed it was the wind picking up and felt relieved that I could now go home with the valid excuse of inclement weather. That was when I heard the first retort. Ten herons are a spectacle but they pale into insignificance when a mixed herd of large male Steller's and California Sea Lions growling and barking respectively are spotted six metres off your bow.

A Steller's bull can weigh up to 1,000 kilos; the California bulls are featherweights at 400 kilos. The Steller's winter along the coast before congregating in the spring at their rookeries (breeding grounds) on islands off the north end of Vancouver Island and south of Haida Gwaii/Queen Charlottes. The Californias come up the coast over the winter, getting fat on herring, before returning to breed on the islands off California. The Californias never used to come up, but now the males are venturing as far as central Vancouver Island, chasing diminishing herring populations. These are the ones that were used in circuses to toss balls on their noses. I hoped there weren't any circus escapees looking for some practice with a canoe.

All sea lions like herring and I was obviously floating unawares over a herring ball. I remained very still and prayed that the fish would find some greener pastures of eel-grass in which to feed. With great barks, splashings and the occasional flipper coming into my view the sea lions dispersed and once again, I was adrift in the void. The only sound was the blood pumping around my body at five times the normal rate.

But the adventure was not over yet. According to the indomitable law of nature, where there is food there are predators, and sea lions are themselves prey to transient pods of Killer Whales or Orcas. Another fact which I can accurately relate is that from a supine position in a canoe, the two-metre dorsal fin of a male Orca is visible from four metres off the stern.

23

I thought, at this stage, that I had run into a transient pod. Transients differ from the residents in a variety of ways, other than being vagrant. The most important difference is that they will hunt sea mammals, whereas the resident ones are content to spend their days eating fish. It was this possibility that alarmed me somewhat from the bottom of my canoe. The method of hunting by these whales is to dive down deep until they see the shadow of the sea lions above them, then race up at break-neck speed and stun the sea lions with their impact. In my nervous state I dwelt upon the fact that the shadows of sea lions and canoes are not widely divergent.

Suddenly, another smaller dorsal fin hove into view and came straight for me. At this stage, I was gripping the gunwales in what might be described as a white-knuckle float. Two males were stationed on either side like sentinels and the smaller female was approaching the canoe slowly. By her side I could make out the small form of a baby close up beside her. About three metres off the stern, they sounded and glided under the canoe so that I had a full view of them. Her dorsal fin grazed the hull and I found myself on my knees praying for the second time that day.

When I calmed down I decided they weren't transients: they were too gregarious and seemed to have the more rounded dorsal fins of the residents. The best way to tell is from their vocalizations under water. Transients are quite silent, and I imagined this lot singing away to themselves as they successfully scared off another errant boater. I paddled home very rapidly in case the heavens were going to lay on a Blue Whale as well. My year passed uneventfully after that and I am quite hopeful that there is still some *communia omnia*.

March

KEEPING ONE EYE OUT FOR THE MURRELETS: THE ANCIENT AND THE MARBLED

There are two sea-bird events going on now on the outer coast but spectators will be hard pressed to keep both eyes open to witness them. It's not that the breeding rituals of our two murrelets (Ancient and Marbled) are boring, it's just that they occur at night and in heaving seas. I saw the arrival of the Ancient Murrelets with one eye. The other eye was trained determinedly on the horizon that was either rising or dropping away from my feet at three metres a second. Both eyes were full of saltwater — the stinging cold water of the Pacific Ocean that pounds the west coast of Haida Gwaii/Queen Charlottes. Through the blur, I could just make out the tiny, black-and-white sea birds that casually ride the swells of a wild March gale.

The crest of every swell as it rises sparkles with a congregation of them, socializing after their long winter in places like Haro and Hecate straits. Three quarters of the world's population of this relative of the puffin arrive on Haida Gwaii to breed at the end of March, and yet only a few suckers for seasickness, saltwater and spruce trees know about them. Unlike puffins, they haven't yet seized the public's imagination and been swept up in our marketing imagery.

It is difficult to seize or sweep up an Ancient Murrelet at the best of times. They spend most of their winters out at sea eating plankton, and their plumage looks much like the skiff of a cresting wave that has caught the light. If you blink, they disappear. They assemble, all 250,000 pairs, on the wildest piece of coastline in British Columbia. They lay their eggs deep in burrows of moss lining the roots of Sitka Spruce on largely inaccessible islands, venturing out only at night to feed. The chicks hatch and within 24 to 48 hours stumble out of their burrows, under cover of the night, to the sea where they quickly disperse with their parents to the open ocean for another year. Even with both eyes open, lying in a dripping rainforest in the middle of the night, it is difficult to spot the balls of fuzz, the baby murrelets, scrambling over the forest floor toward the sea.

Meanwhile, just off the shores nearest the last old-growth rain-forests along the coast from Oregon to Alaska, the Marbled Murrelets are beginning to gather on the water. They are pairing up and acquiring their breeding plumage — a dark-brown, marbled look that will blend in with their nesting habitat of mottled bark and shadows hundreds of feet up in the giant Sitka Spruce and Western Hemlocks. To distinguish a moulting Marbled Murrelet from a piece of driftwood on the crest of a wave with only one eye is tricky at the best of times.

Once they have shed their ocean camouflage of black and white after a winter in the straits, the pairs fly up the river valleys and start circling over the forest canopy in ritual courtship flight. Birds have been clocked at 136 kilometres an hour. By April they will have selected a depression on a huge mossy bough in which to lay the single egg which they both incubate, exchanging duties every 24 hours at dawn until the chick hatches. The adults then step up their duties to eight feeds a day at dusk and dawn. So the only way to witness Marbled Murrelets is to lie on your back in a dripping, old-growth rain-forest in the dark and try to catch a glimpse of a buzz bomb the size of a robin hurtling through the canopy 50 metres above. As a clue, they periodically cry "keer." So few people have seen their nests that it wasn't known where they nested until 1974.

Not surprisingly, with so few people witnessing these birds, their plight has not been well documented. The only time they can be seen around population centres is during the winter in the Salish Sea. But not too many people peer out of ferry windows in November storms. Marbled Murrelet forest is disappearing and safe islets for the Ancient Murrelets are increasingly at risk from introduced species like rats and raccoons. If only murrelets had one tiny fraction of the adver-tising budget of cars or cigarettes, we might get serious about saving them. Just imagine a full-page spread in our popular magazines: "Come to murrelet country." Instead of a herd of cows on a flat savannah with handsome cowboys in spurs chewing their tobacco there would be a flock of murrelets on a wavy sea with beautiful halibut fishermen in gumboots, and one eye on the horizon.

Unfortunately, the advertising world will probably never share this enthusiasm for the murrelet as a powerful icon. It is a great shame since the murrelets need our recognition. They are survivors in a harsh environment; they sail through the air, ride the wild seas and nestle in the ancient forests. They are better symbols of the wild west than a bunch of imported cows and guys with bow legs. Changes to the air, to the sea, to the shoreline or to the forest affect these amazing little birds. Their numbers decline as we move into this last bastion of the wild west. Since getting to know them with both eyes open is virtually impossible, dream a little dream for the murrelets this spring and boycott old-growth timber products.

Nursery Guide to Amphibians and Other Canaries in the Swamp

As you read this hold up your right hand and repeat the following verse:

This little Pacific Treefrog went to the swamp; (wiggle your little finger)
This Red-legged Frog stayed home; (ring finger)
This "blunt-mouthed" salamander ate small bugs; (big finger)
This Bullfrog should have none; (pointer)
And this Roughskin Newt crossed the road safely, all the way to the swamp. (thumb)

In some places you might have to do it secretly. Poetry containing amphibians can get you into trouble; I think they used to burn people for less. But if you can successfully remember this verse, you will have a catchy way of remembering the natural history of some of the more visible aquatic amphibians found in this region.

The Pacific Treefrog is unmistakable in March. The Coast Salish named the month of March after this frog, "Wexes" (a good word for Scrabble). If you live next to a swamp, you will know that it is the season of frenzied hey diddle diddle or

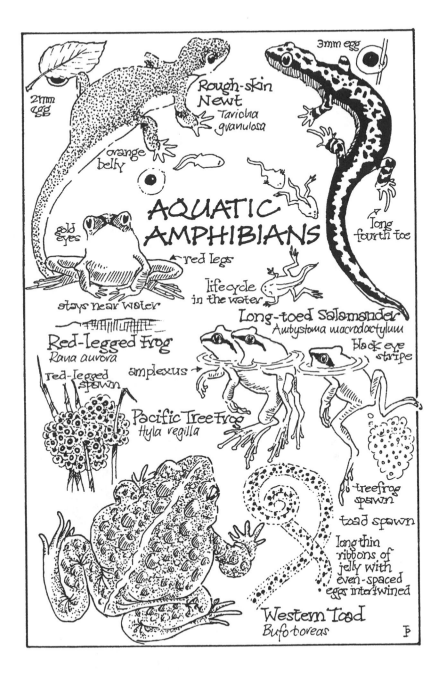

2mm egg

Rough-skin Newt
Taricha granulosa

3mm egg

orange belly

gold eyes

AQUATIC AMPHIBIANS

red legs

long fourth toe

stays near water

lifecycle in the water

Long-toed Salamander
Ambystoma macrodactylum

Red-legged Frog
Rana aurora

red-legged spawn

amplexus →

black eye stripe

Pacific Tree Frog
Hyla regilla

treefrog spawn

toad spawn

long thin ribbons of jelly with even-spaced eggs intertwined

Western Toad
Bufo boreas

"amplexus" — the name for their courting position (also a good word for Scrabble). To demonstrate this might get you into trouble. With the frogs' thin, sensitive skins, the damp, mild weather provides optimum conditions for them to move to the swamps from their trees and breed. "Reck-its" (a loud croak for a frog the size of a little finger) explode from the swamp heralding our most common native frog. They are bright green to brown, depending on their humidity (and mood). They have a distinctive black eye stripe and adhesive disks on the ends of their toes for climbing trees. They lay their eggs around the margins of swamps in loose clumps of jelly.

The Red-legged Frog is a bigger frog (ring finger) whose legs and lower belly are bright red. Their mating chorus is quite soft and they can be elusive, diving down to the bottom of the pond after being spotted. Little Miss Muffet will leap from her tuffet if you sit down beside her. They have clusters of eggs the size of canteloupes and the tadpoles are twice the size of treefrogs. They live by swamps all year round and don't migrate *en masse* to breed.

The "blunt-mouthed" or *Abystoma* salamanders include the finger-sized Long-toed Salamanders, which some coastal nations called more appropriately "Gold-on-the-Back," (easier to spot than their long fourth back toe) and the large Northwestern Salamanders which can grow to the size of your hand. The Long-toed is more wide ranging since it can live in dry as well as wet areas, so it is found throughout the islands of the Salish Sea. Both are elusive because they live underground or deep in decayed logs and only come above ground at night in the rain. These Wee Willie Winkies are best spotted moving to the swamps for breeding. Long-toeds lay large eggs singly in jelly masses the size of a plum that are attached to stems or leaves. Northwesterns produce egg masses the size of a grapefruit. They are usually in shallow water less than half a metre deep. The larvae look like Little Bo-Peep with their three ostrich-plume gills on each side.

When you get to "bullfrog," shake your pointing finger up and down and wear a stern expression. American Bullfrogs (the noise they make is a loud drone) have spread from the east to the west via the ice-cream pails of junior biologists. These are big frogs and unlikely to be confused with any native species except maybe Western Toads, which deserve an entire poem on their own. The toad has rough warty skin, unlike the frog. Toads lay their eggs in strings, not clusters. Bullfrogs are like many of the invasive species on the coast: beautiful in their own right but they completely decimate other species. They are even known to eat ducklings and junior biologists. All the king's horses and all the king's men can't put these ecosystems back together again. Don't release bullfrogs in any of our lakes.

Finally, my favourite, the Roughskin Newt, as fat and long as your thumb and palm. These grand old dukes (duchesses) of the swamp are currently on the march (slowly) to their breeding swamps. The most common viewing is on a road between swamp and forest where they customarily get run over by unobservant motorists. They are not Jack be nimble, Jack be quicks until they get into the water. My faith in humanity is restored when I see an adult swerve for a newt. They have bright orange bellies, rough brown backs and humanoid toes. Their amplexus is balletic with tender groping. They deposit eggs on the undersides of leaves close to the surface and the jelly is very thin. Some races of these newts are rumoured to have tetradotoxins in their skin which is the same ingredient as witchdoctors use for making zombies — living dead. Those who squish newts might consider the possibility of newt revenge.

The rhyme done, you can lie back and listen to the chorus of the treefrog. "Rock-a-bye baby with the treefrog." The nightly lullaby fulfills our primal longing for the swamp and intellectually reassures us that amphibians have lived to breed another season. The presence of amphibians indicates well-being in the ecosystem since their skins absorb water, oxygen and all substances therein. Amphibians are referred to as the "canaries in the swamp" with their loss preceding a greater ecological collapse. With the world losing amphibians and their habitat at an alarming rate we should know that when Jack falls down and breaks his crown, Jill comes tumbling after.

In response, the International Union for the Conservation of Nature has organized a "Task Force on Declining Amphibian

Populations." There are active groups setting up monitoring programs and they can always do with some swamp watchers to monitor amphibians. Locate a local swamp or pond and observe the area for the various amphibians. The ones in the nursery rhyme all have an aquatic phase in spring when they breed, so this is the best time of the year to observe the adults. Look for the eggs and/or the larvae (e.g., tadpoles) later on in the spring.

Traditional poetry on amphibians is voluminous. They were the symbol of life, Kings of the World, Mother Goddesses for every culture until the New Testament and Mother Goose when they became equated with unclean spirits. Probably those desert dwellers and pastoralists didn't know how to relate to amphibians and we ended up with rhymes about this little piggie.

SPLASHES TO SPLASHES AND GRUNTS TO GRUNTS: A TWENTY-FOUR HOUR TRIBUTE TO SPRING

I have never read a tribute to spring that starts off in the dark with lots of grunting, at least not the polite ones. Odes to spring usually start off with sun-washed daffodils bursting out of the poet's mouth or some bumblebees buzzing around in a pastoral torpor. This tribute to spring begins in the pitch black, somewhere near a herring ball in the Salish Sea. The ferry engines were throbbing, diesel fumes hung over the deck and I could only just make out the tops of the whitecaps, stony grey in the black night. Normally, in these conditions it would seem a little overenthusiastic to rush to the side of the ferry with a pair of binoculars but I and 12 Boy Scouts did just that. Although I had my binoculars and they had their slingshots, the vernal impulse was the same. Out of the black came the grunts and splashes of a herd of sea lions in crazed pursuit of those silver darlings of spring — the Pacific Herring.

There is no mistaking the pursuit of a herring ball by a large, hungry herd of one-ton Steller's Sea Lions with a few California Sea Lions thrown in for good measure. The noise overrides the throb of a ferry engine and nothing will stop them in their path. This was a reassuring notion since I felt ill-prepared to give a nurturing motherhood lecture in the dark to a pack of spring-fevered Boy Scouts with only my binoculars for self defence. When even the captain couldn't plough in his ship through the thick of them, I realized that here was an indomitable force and that spring had arrived with a splash.

The next morning, I awoke to a smell that, like the arrival of the herring, gets the blood rushing around my brain. The morning was calm and clear, and the sun had started to warm up the earth, creating a little Turkish steam bath of pleasure. This was getting onto ground more akin to the classic images of spring: breathing in the raw oxygen of budding plants; revelling in the bright greens of new growth; thinking pure thoughts of brightness and the sweetness of new life. Those kind of thoughts that can even make you remember fondly an entire troop of Boy Scouts. This is the mood in which I approached my first Indian-plum of the year.

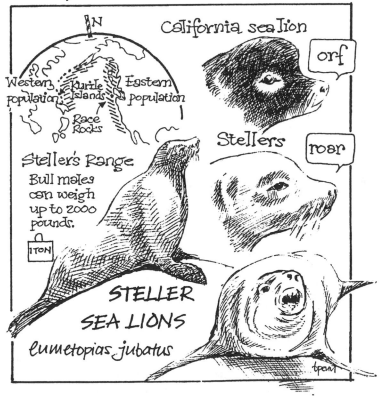

Smelling the first Indian-plum is a spiritual experience. All around the Salish Sea, in wetter areas where we haven't ravaged the native plants, there are examples of this early blooming wild shrub that bursts into bud around now and floods the air with a delicate scent. Some would argue that the smell is not fragrant but closer to the urine of a tomcat; it seems to be a personal matter. The flowers emerge before the leaves do and look like an Indian princess — that's the story anyway and somewhat ironic, because the Salish people used this shrub as a purgative. It's called the "clean-out-everything-inside" shrub. Which — if we are really making a tribute to spring — is quite a necessary part of the ritual.

Keeping this in mind, careful not to chew on the Indian-plum, I remained in a thicket and listened for the next signal of spring — the call of the Song Sparrow. If you want to learn only one bird call, this should be it. Some day you'll be walking down a street with the anxieties of the world upon you and suddenly three clear notes (two low, then one high) followed by a trill will interrupt your thoughts. There on a shrub in the midst of the madness will be a little male sparrow singing his heart out, announcing the start of spring. You'll never forget it once you hear it and spring will always be that much sweeter — especially if you are a female Song Sparrow.

From my thicket, I was settling in for my first snooze in the sun when the unmistakable call of a pair of American Oystercatchers broke my reverie. I'll stop doing almost anything to listen to those first gleeful cries of courting oystercatchers. These birds are worse than Boy Scouts for drawing attention to themselves. They have a piercing sort of "wheep" whistle that carries a long way over the water. They have a bill that looks like a carrot in their mouth, bright red eyes in a tiny head, and long, pink legs which fork out in strange directions from under their all-black bodies. Their endearing quality of announcing themselves is also their downfall.

Oystercatchers are ground nesters on rocky islets and isolated shorelines but are now rare because they often fail to raise their one or two young to maturity. Some well-meaning kayaker or naturalist visits the rocky islet, puts the parents off the nest, they cry, and wham! a lurking seagull or eagle carries off the egg or chick. Pairs were failing to raise a chick year after year until a watch patrol near our islets was set up by locals. Now, as soon as the courting behaviour starts, kayakers are fended off with signs, motherhood lectures and Boy Scouts. That day in the thicket, as I heard the indomitable optimism in their call, I could finally share it.

The afternoon progressed and a few more tributes to spring were lining up to fill my fountain. Somewhere about six o'clock, as the sun gently collapsed into the sea, I saw a Little Brown Bat dart out from a big fir and scoop up an early moth. The insects were emerging and their predators were following. Bats are quick to come out of their semi-hibernation if it is a warm evening. I think they hear the flip of the herring tails, the grunt of the sea lions and the trill of the sparrow. If the bats made an appearance, then another familiar group was sure to appear. Sure enough, within a few seconds of nightfall, another type of grunt and bark began. It was the chorus of the male Pacific Treefrog, warming up to a deafening climax of croaks to lure the females into the swamp with a splash. Like the sea lions after the herring, they will drown out everything and single-mindedly pursue their rites of spring.

And thus my tribute to spring begins in the dark with grunts and splashes, and ends in the dark with grunts and splashes.

SEE WEED OR SEAWEED?

There are at least 1,001 popular uses of seaweed. There are also at least 1,001 reasons why the best use of seaweed might be to leave it where you find it. Seaweed is in the air right now as it is the season of low daytime tides, and a veritable army is heading off for the tangles and beds of seaweeds, dragging their black garbage bags, anchors and other paraphernalia across them. Various seaweed advocates have been questioning what kind of impact the collection or disturbance of seaweed has on the ecology of the sea. After asking everyone I can find who has some opinion upon the topic, I have come to the conclusion that seaweed advocacy is an uphill struggle. It is complicated, there is not a lot of information on seaweed ecology and one is having to broach the issues with two prickly groups — gardeners and yachtsmen.

There seem to be two clear issues at heart: disturbance of living eel-grass beds and kelp forests through dredging, anchors and trampling, and carrying off the tangle of seaweed on the shoreline. Discussing alternatives to clearcut logging with timber companies is a piece of Rockweed cake, compared to discussing alternatives to dredging and anchoring in eel-grass beds with yachting groups. Meanwhile, gardeners have been hauling seaweed onto their gardens for thousands of years to enrich the soil, and there doesn't seem to be much reason to stop. The main arguments in defence of the seaweed are the very reasons why the soil gets enriched — actually 1,001 of them. Seaweeds are magnets for a diversity of species.

After many years of trying to defend local underdogs such as Roughskin Newts, Northern Alligator Lizards and Death Camas, I must admit that Bull Kelp and other algaes offer the greatest

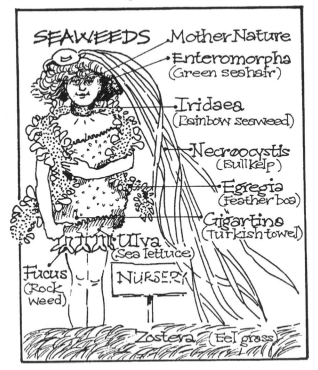

public relations challenge yet. Imagine the scene: a new algae advocate, first day on the job, wading purposefully through the mud, clams squirting water up your shorts, and you casually mention to the large, dahlia experts with the sharpened shovels that the delicate *Ulva* (also known as Sea Lettuce) is best left undisturbed. When they have finished laughing and eyeing the damp clam stains on your shorts, you are forced to reappraise your technique and devise something more conducive to success.

These are additional opening lines that I have tried and found not to be successful:

"Good afternoon. Did you know that there are more seaweeds along the west coast than just about anywhere else in the world (600 to be exact) and that 34 of them grow nowhere else in the world and what the hell do you think you're doing removing them even if they *are* lying on the beach?"

"What a lovely day we're having. Did you know that what you're raking up is the restaurant of the beach, the diner of diatoms, the sushi bar for sandhoppers and shorebirds, the paradise of periwinkles, the nursery of salmon, the harbinger of herring and the sunscreen of the shore? Yes, I can appreciate that seaweed advocates make good compost too but ..."

"Hello. You must be a gardener? Don't tell anyone else but I have learned that Scotch Broom and English Ivy well-mulched are far more effective as a fertilizer than any seaweed yet discovered. I wouldn't want this to get out, mind you, in case the supply runs out."

"I can see that it is very important to scrape the paint off your boat in this eel-grass bed but have you ever pondered the effect of anti-fouling paint on the populations of Stalked Jellyfish which live amongst the fronds? No, you haven't. Well, maybe Skeleton Shrimp then? No, how about Penpoint Gunnels?"

"Hello, hello, up there in the 81-metre yacht *Sargasso Weed*, this is the HMS Courageous speaking from the rowboat below. I just wondered if you could possibly arrange for your crew to lift up that 200-kilo anchor that has just ploughed a furrow two metres deep through the Giant Kelp forest and maybe drop it somewhere east of Kamachatka. I've heard they have some lovely cruise-ship docks to tie up to."

"I'm sorry to bother you, but did you know that you just picked up a Rockweed biflagellate male gamete sperm on its way to fertilize a non-motile female gamete liberated from its oogonium which through a process of snygamy results in a diploid cell which can then again become a conspicuous, free-living generation ready for maturity?"

It is hard to put forward the case to protect seaweeds. They are prolific, productive plants that seem to be irrepressible. They are relatively unstudied and we are only just piecing together the relationships within the eel-grass meadows and kelp forests. We have very little understanding of the impact of removing seaweed that is washed up on the tide line. And despite the fact that we have few common names for seaweeds, the uses we put them to run deeply into our culture.

As children, we use the long stalk of the Bull Kelp, which can grow up to 60 centimetres a day, to skip — clinging, on one end, to the brain-like anchor and at the other to the float bladder. Who has not popped the bladders of Rockweed (a species of *Fucus*), eaten Sea Lettuce (one of the *Ulva* species), gasped at the irridescent flashes of Rainbow Seaweed (one of the *Iridaea* species) or giggled at Sea-condoms (*Coilodesme californica*)? As adults, we hang out in sushi bars munching Japanese Nori seaweed, mulch our gardens with Rockweed and still giggle at Sea-condoms.

As for me, on the way to my wedding, I used the top of the kelp as a veil, put on Green Sea Hair (species of *Enteromorpha*), draped a Feather Boa Kelp (*Egregia menziesii*) and a skimpy Turkish Towel (*Gigartina exasperata*) around myself as a wedding garment before my mother (*Gigantic exasperata*) forced me into pantyhose and dress.

This helped lead me to my final conclusion: there are some uses of seaweed more helpful to the wide community of shore-line species than others. Now when I go down to the sea and spot the large dahlia expert or the Captain Sargasso ploughing through the seaweed, I ask them if they want to hold each end of the kelp while I skip up and down in nothing but *Egregia menziesii* and *Gigartina exasperata*. Works every time.

April

THE GOOD, THE DRAB AND THE MUDDY:
BRANT GEESE AND GUMBOOT WEARERS

It was the party in the dungeon that convinced me. Brant — black geese — attract a special type of follower. Every April I go to some party somewhere in honour of this small goose. It is a custom, a strange connection to a seemingly unremarkable bird. Brant are almost plain geese that spend their summers nesting up in the arctic tundra from Alaska to Siberia and their winters hanging around eel-grass beds in southerly saltmarshes and estuaries. Some travel up and down the Pacific coast wintering in the Baja; some travel up and down the Atlantic wintering on the North American side or the European side. In the spring and autumn, flocks of Brant land on the eel-grass beds in between — known in birdtalk as staging points — to rest and refuel.

Whenever flocks of Brant arrive, groups of people seem to spontaneously flock as well. Brant fans are characterized by drab green clothing to blend in with the eel-grass. Anyone with binoculars and telescopes draped over every shoulder is also suspect. They all are seized by a passionate need to watch the long, irregular strings of geese winging low across the horizon; it's some primal urge, a throwback to a time when the arrival of the Brant meant a full stomach and a new feather pillow. Brant (called "Brent geese" in Britain) are as eagerly anticipated on the coasts of this continent as they are in Europe and Russia. In fact, the Brant that nest together up in the eastern arctic split themselves between Canada and Britain — true internationalists.

Which leads me back to the dungeon party. I was in Northern Ireland a few years ago in April with an international gathering of Brant-/Brentophiles celebrating the arrival of the geese *en route* to their nests in the arctic. It was held in a dungeon that was owned by Lady Something-or-other. It was suitably spacious to hold the flock of us — drab green clothing, gumboots and telescopes. It was very difficult to tell the Canadians from the Irish or the Russians, as they all spoke the same bird language. The

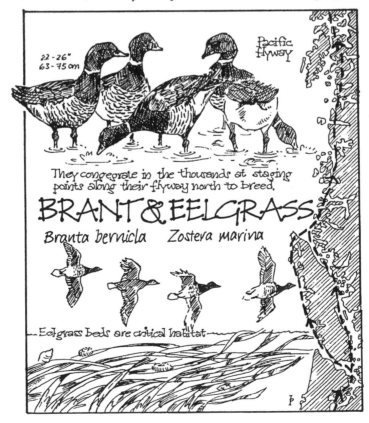

22-26"
63-75 cm

Pacific Flyway

They congregate in the thousands at staging points along their flyway north to breed.

BRANT & EELGRASS

Branta bernicla   Zostera marina

Eelgrass beds are critical habitat

dungeon housed a fantastic collection of hunting implements and skins of extinct or nearly extinct animals collected by an ancestor of Lady So-and-so. Her affinity for wildlife was obviously a genetic trait. Sitting on a moth-eaten polar-bear skin, chatting to a Gaelic-speaking Brent enthusiast, I told him about the various Brant festivals on the coast.

"We don't have dungeons in North America as yet," I remarked, "although our malls could be described as such. Every April when the geese arrive we don our gumboots, gather in church halls and chat about the state of our eel-grass beds. We hang up paintings of the geese and try and persuade the other members of the community that hanging around in drab green clothing with implements around your neck is a suitable and admirable occupation. Then we try and persuade the Lords of the Council that eel-grass beds are preferable to mini-golf courses, trailer parks, new piers for cruise ships and pink condominiums." My Gaelic-speaking friend was utterly sympathetic and said that they had been having the same problem for about one thousand years.

The nice thing about these festivals is that there is lots of positive encouragement. Brant/Brent were nearly extinct 60 years ago throughout their range in the northern hemisphere. Thanks to the persistence of all these remarkable people, who want to continue to watch them fly in at dusk with the light glinting on their white tail feathers and their gentle honking to each other, many of the staging points have been protected. Numbers of Brant are holding their own. So if you feel like being amongst a flock, travel to Brant staging areas along the coast and join the throng. Don't forget your drab clothing.

TEMPTATION IN THE OAK MEADOWS: RESISTANCE IN THE LAWNS

This is a two-part piece. You read Part 1 to get relaxed, then Part 2 to get fired up — sort of like a sauna. Part 1 is my attempt at a "visual imaging exercise" — the kind of story that they read in yoga classes to a background of monks chanting. I recommend a loud bagpipe myself.

PART 1: TEMPTATION IN THE OAK MEADOWS

It is time to go into the wilderness over the next 40 days and get tempted. The ancient Garry Oak meadows of the dry, south-facing shores of the Salish Sea are blooming. Before you cross to the wild side, there is an old ritual that must be carried out. Pass the soles of your feet over a Maidenhair Fern and touch the discarded skin of a Wandering Garter Snake. The former causes you to dance lightly upon the earth and the latter will make you irresistible.

Temptations are out there aplenty, at least in the biblical sense. Imagine soaking up the dew through your frost-shattered cheeks as you lie with the decadent purple Satin-flowers and glittering Spring-gold. Let the Blue-eyed-Mary put the sparkle back in your eyes. Climb under the fallen winter branches and drape yourself in sensuous fungi, luscious lichens and mosses so luxuriant that they caress your skin. Imagine abandoning yourself inside the nest of the Bushtit. Strut with the California Quails, black head-plumes bobbing. Circle with the Red-tailed Hawks looking for foolhardy voles. Tiptoe through the nun-like Easter Lilies as if you've entered a holy place. You have — they are fewer and more sacred than churches.

The Turkey Vultures have arrived and are casting mysterious shadows across your body. The male Rufous Hummingbirds are spreading the seed of the Red-flowering Currants. Violet-green Swallows are coursing through the sky in sinful figure-of-eights. Purple Finches are taking their pleasure to the tops of trees, their purple passion exploding with the Broad-leaved Shootingstars below — more passions are reflected by the delicate Sea-blush back to your cheeks. Fritter away an afternoon of decadence amongst the *Fritillaria* love-plant — the Chocolate Lily, a bell of brown and white petals entwined forever.

Imagine getting drunk on the sea of camas-blue — the flower that launched wars and fed nations. Sin in the camas meadows comes in various forms. Feasting amongst the edible Common Camas and the Great Camas, you play Russian roulette with the white Death Camas. One wrong bite with forbidden fruit and you might die.

A symbol of Easter & rebirth. Found on the shores of the Salish Sea on grassy knolls.

yellow anthers

white

paired mottled leaves

Also known as Fawn Lily

EASTER LILY
Erythronium oregonum

Basking in the light of a warm sun that seeps onto a rocky promontory, you return your irresistible charm to the garter snake. With the dew of the fern still drying on your soles, you float over these magnificent tempting meadows and leave nothing but a sigh over the Salish Sea.

PART 2: RESISTANCE IN THE LAWNS

To those of you who have strong affection for a lawn, I think you should know that there's been a bit of a mistake. Lawns are an illusion of a bored old monk of 12th-century Britain. He was the guy who was first ordered to paint Camelot, the Garden of Eden and Paradise for some errant knights looking for redemption. Imagine him in a grey, damp cell, one drippy

43

summer, gazing out over an old pasture full of cows, crumbling castles and tyrannical kings with the threat of eternal damnation on his head if the goods aren't produced. What does he do but reach for his little pot of bright green paint and just turn that cow pasture into Eden.

With one stroke of a brush he wipes away the mud, the poop and the plants and creates a smooth green lawn for the damsels to dally on. With a little bit of chromium oxide and egg yolk he reduces the complexity of a piece of earth to a monoculture, and inextricably links our perceptions of Paradise with a lawn. The idea caught on and the lawn has become the holiest artifact ever to cross the ocean. Eight hundred years later, we are still dallying around with that image in our mind, and ploughing up millions of acres of the real Paradise because of it.

Few things are as blasphemous as the challenge of the lawn; people will give up their cars and children before their lawns. Yet lawns rank up there with clearcut logging and uranium mining as one of the great mistakes of western civilization. Most of us can feel relatively righteous about cleansing ourselves of clearcut logging or uranium mining; we'll use our blue boxes and avoid nuclear reactors. But who can truthfully say that they have not enjoyed the pleasures of the lawn at some stage in their life? That gentle, friendly, idyllic place that we crawled upon as babies, played ball upon as children, lazed upon as adults. That sultry midsummer smell of cut grass and steaming moisture as the sprinklers lazily rocked back and forth. The myth of the lawn as the place of eternal youth and summer. The green slopes around one's castle.

Milton talks about lawns in Paradise. William Morris wrote "she came where that lawn of the woods lay wide in the flood of light." We suck it all in, those subtle contrasts of light on an even carpet of green, the hint of soft romance on the lawn. Our imported muses and artists echoed these sentiments. Who could resist this mythology? Who could leave such a precious idea behind and forego the pleasures of recreating the Garden of Eden in a land 10,000 miles away?

Of course, this little illusion has not been without its promoters. What entrepreneur wouldn't spot the potential to exploit this myth? Imagine an entire population devoted to the idea of lawns landing in a new environment that has dry summers, completely different flora, fauna, terrain, soil and weather, with a whole lot of money and looking for creative alternatives to grazing sheep in their front yard. Klondike nothing — the smart ones headed out of the hills and set up lawn shops.

I once opened up a flyer from a lawn shop entitled "Lawn Care." First we had Health Care, now we have Lawn Care. It amounts to the same thing: a barrage of chemicals, quick-fixes and weaponry that can serve up Paradise on a silver tray. Counting up the totals of the gadgets, herbicides, pesticides and fertilizers, I realized that if one bought every article in the ad they could spend an incredible $5,429.65 on their lawn, after the capital costs of constructing it. This is more than twice what is spent per capita on health care. Any economist would argue this is the stuff that fuels our economy, the purchase of non-essential items for non-essential things. If this is the stuff that fuels our economy, let us pray for the return of manure.

We are not the only victims of the Great Lawn Delusion: the real victims are the involuntarily displaced residents who lived in the place where the lawn is now. A vital community of messy, wild, seemingly disordered plants and animals, not to mention the terrain, soil and weather. First we flatten the terrain, change the soil and alter the weather (by global warming), then we stick down these rolls of imported turf over the homes of the plants and animals. We transform a rich, interesting, lively piece of earth into a lawn that has the biological diversity of a shag rug. There has got to be more to Paradise than a shag rug.

Back between the eight pages of unrecycled, pulped-old-growth "Lawn Care," I counted 27 pounds of dubious chemicals that were available for purchase. Chemicals that, no matter how you look at them, do more damage than a host of rampaging knights. Then, not content with poisoning everything, we will drain all our rivers and reservoirs to keep our lawns green. Despite knowing that most of us live in the rain shadow of the Olympics and water is a limited resource, we pour vast amounts of the stuff on our lawns just for the sheer pleasure of expending more resources and energy to mow it.

In this regard, I have a small conspiracy theory. Perhaps the whole lawn thing is a monastic plot to punish all those happy little damsels and knights who did naughty things on the lawn. Forever more their heirs are banished to a punishing Sunday routine on sprinklers, mowers and weedeaters — those whirling, noisy, diabolical things that slice every living thing in their path in pursuit of a flawless lawn. Like Health Care, perhaps we need a return to an acceptance of natural processes like birth, growing and dying without resorting to Mr. Weed and Feed to assist us at every turn.

Now traditions die hard. I will go on record as saying that try as I may, I cannot quite get lawns out of my system. So, what I have done is designate a small patch of monoculture over to my overwhelming cultural inheritance. The rest of the piece of earth that I am lucky enough to rest upon for a while is being restored to its former inhabitants. It is a slow, painful business. It requires doing nothing most of the time, then occasionally playing god and weeding out errant European introductions. I feel a colonial cleansing of guilt as I grab a Scotch Broom or English Ivy by the roots and throttle it. There are 800 years of delusion to overcome. But I have a picture in my mind — it is of an artist, sitting gazing out over my restored Garry Oak wild-flower meadow full of Easter Lilies, Sea-blush, Broad-leaved Shootingstars, Spring-gold, Satin-flowers, Western Buttercups, Chocolate Lilies and Blue-eyed-Mary one spring day, listening to bagpipes and painting Paradise.

GO THOU TO THE ANT: A THOUSAND DOGMAS SNIFF AT A HUMBLE INSECT

This might not seem like earth-shaking news but it is: a species of ant, recently discovered in the wilds of Papua New Guinea, is a social parasite living in the nests of others. This is terribly exciting to all those who are mildly weary of social commentators insisting we all should be "as industrious as ants." Projecting human values onto other animals is fine sport but even finer when a little extra information muddies the waters.

Ants have been used tiresomely since the Ming Dynasty to justify every dogma of the day. Monarchist? Ants have it all: queens, nobles and commoners. Capitalist or Calvinist? Even the Bible will tell you to "Go to the ant, thou sluggard, consider her ways and be wise." Socialist or communist? Every ant works tirelessly for the common good. And now at last my own partic-ular favourite dogma — social parasitism — well served by a species of ant.

I have long had hopes that the ant would see me through. My belief stemmed from the obvious contradiction that the Bible failed to point out: to "go to the ant" and "consider her ways," you have to be as much of a "sluggard" as other non-capitalists in the streets staring at the pavement.

I spent much of my childhood staring at pavements, watching ants and being a social parasite. It was such a natural state of affairs to be doing nothing but watching them that it never entered my mind that I should aspire to be like one. I had a particular fondness for black-and-red Western Thatching Ants. They're the ones that sting, and live in nest mounds made out of the thatch (pine needles, leaf skeletons, wood debris) that carpets Douglas-fir forests.

We had a thatch mound in our back garden and ant trails used to go over our stone wall. If I lay on my stomach I could see these insects in stunning detail. All day the ants would scurry back and forth, picking up stuff, dropping stuff and changing direction erratically. During the hottest part of the day they would travel in shady sections and in the coolest part they would travel in the sun. You could get them to go where you wanted by creating a moving umbrella with your hand. I

THATCHING ANTS
Formica obscuripes
nest mound
red heads & black bodies

would try to corner ants, head them off in different directions, capture them and release them on brothers, bribe them with Twinkie crumbs or dead flies or even feed them to each other. This was the start of behavioural experiments that have served me well into child rearing.

Over time, I have had the opportunity to lounge like a sluggard around many colonies and I came upon a huge one this week, in full activity, exciting me once again on the topic of ants. During the course of my observations and reading up on the subject I have discovered that even our homegrown *Formica obscuripes* have rich analogies for most of our millennium crises, including unemployment, corporatization and the battle of the sexes.

For a start, the thatching ant colonies have three castes: one queen, a few winged males and thousands of sterile female workers. The men lie around waiting to fly away with the hatching virgin queens in June. Sterile, wingless females make up the vast proportion of the colony, which in a big thatch can be up to a quarter of a million individuals. No doubt this will seem the perfect homily, as either a threat or a promise for the future.

As far as social organization goes, there are outside workers and inside workers. The outside workers don't live as long as the inside ones but they get to gather food, chop down plants with their big mandibles and defend the thatch (remember, they are female too). The penalties for the inside workers are that they have to clean the nest and tend the babies. This division of labour and associated values might go some way to explaining why there are differences between rural and urban communities, and both sides should be reminded that in a crisis, such as a flood, all workers band together to save the nest.

It is easy enough to analyze any of these analogies for yourself, although spotting a thatching ant nest in a Douglas-fir forest is not as easy as it sounds. Often the first hint that you're near a nest is the sensation of a hundred little jaws sinking into your flesh with formic acid (the root of their Latin name) stinging the wound.

If you want to find a thatching ant nest, look for mounds of needles or follow a trail of red-and-black ants. They prefer dry, well-drained, untrampled parts of the forest with a sunny aspect where there is not a great deal of undergrowth, usually at the base of a tree. Lie around, thou sluggard, consider their ways and be wise. Wise to what I am not really sure — something is bound to come to mind. Maybe you'll discover a new species of ant that searches endlessly for a social organization that works. Or maybe you'll just discover the joy of the warmer spring days.

FLYING CIRCUS: HUMMINGBIRDS UNDER THE BIG TOP

I ran away to the circus today. I wanted to join the sequinned trapeze artists and clowns walking the tightrope. They are good company, they like life on the edge and don't hide their exuberance. It didn't take me long. My bags were packed within seconds: a flask of sugared water, a pillow and a spyglass. The journey was short: out the front door, along the verandah, down the creaking stairs and into the bush which starts modestly with a patch of hedge nettles. Somewhere around the Red-flowering Currants I found their encampment. I poured a wee drink for myself from my flask, then filled the hummingbird feeder, swinging like a trapeze under the big top cedar.

It goes to your head, this one-part-sugar, three-parts-water stuff. You start talking to hummingbirds if you drink too much. I was in a mood for drinking. A virus had run the gamut through me, my children, the car, the computer and the water pump. Too many exuberances were bottled up. "You are lucky," I yelled at the ringmaster. "You just turn up in this currant patch after a winter down south, dressed to the nines in a costume of red sequins, then play host to some greatest-show-on-earth." I shut up when the show began in earnest.

I shifted onto my back as the drumroll started. It isn't exactly a drumroll — it's a buzzing courtship display and the suspense is far greater. First there is the diminishing buzz as the male climbs up the arc of the ellipse toward the sun. The buzz fades to almost a bee's hum as he reaches the top of his ellipse, then there is a hummingbird's-breath-of-a-pause followed by the return descent. I don't know if I can describe — with the greatest of ease — what it feels like to be directly under the nadir of the arc of an invisible trapeze carrying a circus freak in sequins. Like all good entertainment it is a catharsis of ill humours. (Cathars, from the same Greek root, were medieval monks trying to achieve purity.) My little cathar repeated his performance five or six times before the next acts.

The next two acts followed quickly. Feeding and mating — they are sometimes indistinguishable — are a cross between a clown show and lion taming. They are so raw, it makes my own life look like a tea party. Food fights expose hummingbirds as the true freaks that they are. They are in outrageous little bodies that need to eat half their weight in sugar daily. To do this their hearts have to beat 1,000 times a minute, their lungs exhale 250

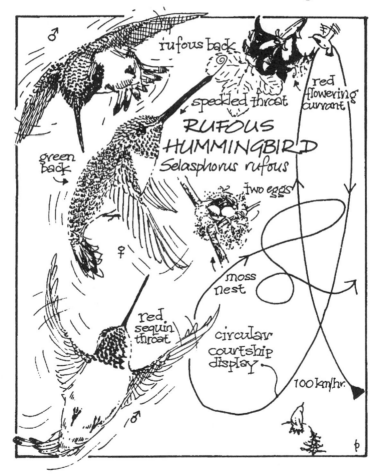

breaths per minute, their long tongues lick flowers 780 times a minute and their wings beat 12,000 times a minute. How any organism could have evolved to do so many things, so quickly, all at once, makes them the strangest-show-on-earth.

With my spyglass I can see them close up, fighting over the sweet stuff. "Cheers, my dears," I call out from below. "Thank goodness I only need a couple of glasses of this stuff to keep my heart beating."

Meanwhile the clowns go at it. They advance, they attack, they pummel. No one is spared: men, women, children. The females are as ferocious as the males — just green sequins on their back with no red ones to flirt with. The dowdy young of the first brood are driven away to go start their own circus. The males pummel the females into a coupling that makes their wings seem inert. Three weeks later the next brood will hatch out under the big top Western Redcedar-bough nest and three weeks after that they'll be fledged. This is life on the tightrope. Lose your food supply, too many cold days, get a virus, lose the fight and it's all over.

"Ha," I exhale from my comfortable position on my pillow below, "you drew the short straw," I continue sipping from my flask, "living life on the edge," — as I wave my finger three times a minute — "living so dangerously," the thought slowly enters my mind, "living so excitingly ...." When the circus leaves town this summer, look for me — the gaudy trapeze lady with the green sequin suit.

BUDDHA AND THE BUTTERFLIES: SEARCH FOR THE TEN MOST WANTED

I'm saddling up Esmeralda, my old bike, this week for a special mission. I'm going to track down the Ten Most Wanted. I won't be looking for the bad guys — though I might bump into a few where I'm going. My mission is to look for the ten endangered butterflies of the Salish Sea. Their only crime is that they are disappearing without telling us. My reward is a pleasant flutter around rare native wildflower meadows. Equipment for this event includes a comfortable bike, an inflatable raft and a good picnic hamper. The tone of the day will be a cross between a Buddhist retreat and a Sherlock Holmes plot. The Zen of sleuthing. Buddha once said of butterflies, "From you I have learned more than from all the writings of the Brahmans." Sherlock Holmes' axiom is that "the little things are infinitely the most important." The success of the trip will not be to drag home the bodies but to observe some of these treasures at first hand.

Although I haven't quite finished the complete set of Brahman writings, I feel they will have to be good to compete with the life history of the butterfly. Life begins for this insect as a tiny egg anchored to its host plant. Hatching into a many-footed gelati-

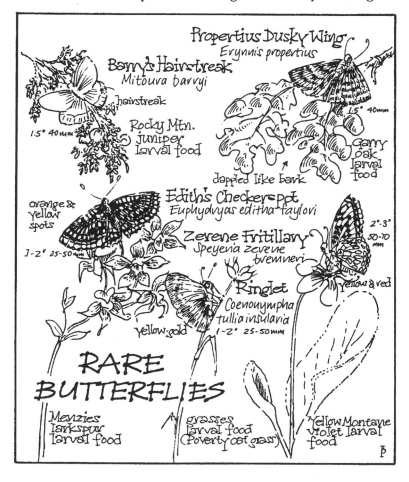

nous mass, the caterpillar gorges itself upon the plant, then spins itself a cocoon of silk and turns into a pupa. While in its cocoon, it undergoes a transformation in which its cells dissolve into a primeval living soup, then reassemble into a multi-coloured flying insect. The butterfly emerges and finds its mate (probably through the wing pattern) and has a delicate courtship. It detects its host plant through its smelling antennae, feasts upon the nectar and lays its eggs on that same succulent flower before dying. Butterflies "transcend" from the dependent infant stage, through an exploratory, indulgent adolescence to a quiet, dignified maturity full of beauty and purposefulness. Unfortunately, like humans, the middle phase is the longest.

This time of year marks the metamorphosis of many caterpillars into their brief adult butterfly form. They are all currently fluttering around, hatching, feeding, courting and revealing the truths of the universe. One truth of the universe is that if you remove the specific host plants, the butterflies disappear. Not surprisingly, we have ten threatened ones here, all of whose host plants grow in the native meadows. Hence my mission, to see if some of them are still around.

Esmeralda and I begin our adventure on a south-sloping mountainside, where Garry Oaks grow, in search of the Propertius Duskywing. This butterfly's larval food is the oak so it is inextricably bound to the tree. Over an inch long, this moth-like creature camouflages beautifully with the bark, so look carefully for the white scaling on its dusky wings. Each wing is covered by thousands of these tiny little scales. Lie flat on your back and gaze steadfastly into the gnarled boughs of the tree. Many butterflies of various origins will float by. Don't trouble yourself if you have not sorted out the duskywing from other errant ones. After some years, I'm told, the distinctions will become obvious.

If you are very lucky, you might just spot some bluish butterflies hovering around rare wild pea species. There are two endangered "blue" butterflies — the Greenish and the Icaroides Blue. When you have had enough of trying to imagine what Icaroides Blue might look like, reach for your picnic basket and get out an Avocado Green and a Peach Blush. Gently feast upon the nectar and flutter down the mountain to the rocky shores.

Isolated coastal rocky bluffs are good places to find large patches of stonecrop flowers, a cactus-like plant where Moss' Elfin will be hovering. These elfin butterflies are two-toned brown on the underside and mahogany on the topside, with a white border. They lay their eggs on the buds of this succulent plant. Where there are undisturbed stonecrops, there are elfins. Unfortunately, some shore landowners haven't read Buddha so these places are becoming rare.

I have to leave Esmeralda and get into the canoe to spot Barry's Hairstreak, a little tailed butterfly, or the elusive Ringlet. The hairstreak larvae feed on the Rocky Mountain juniper which grows sporadically on ungrazed Salish Sea islets in the lusher spots. The small, velvety, ochre-yellow Ringlet loves native fescue grasses in damp pockets but not the Kentucky blue grass and sprinklers found in modern yards. If you can't find either amidst the mono-species turf, remember that one of Sherlock Holmes' villains came to a sticky end in a moor for killing butterflies.

The next three on the most wanted list might require one more additional piece of equipment — a friendly lepidopterist to help you find them. I had to take a lepidopterist on my handlebars to remote places to find Zerene's Fritillary amongst the Yellow Montane Violets and Edith's Checkerspot amongst the Menzies' Larkspur. Exhausted by our effort, and out of Peach Blush, we only gazed at Mount Finlayson near Victoria where the last Chalcedon Checkerspot was spotted a few decades ago.

The tenth butterfly also evoked something of a pilgrimage, as we had to go back to the ancient Salish village site of Songhees, Victoria. It is the spot where the last Large Marble was seen at the turn of the century. There is a remote chance that a population of this species (that I hope doesn't look like its name), unique to the region, is still lurking unsuspected. I hold out a hope that they might return because the corollary of Sherlock's axiom is that if we look out for the little things, then everything else important will follow.

May

FLIGHT OF THE DRAGONS

If you walk along a road today, dream about flying dragons. Close your eyelids, heavy from the dull glare of hot car roofs and look for irridescent blues, greens, yellows and reds darting in the moist air. Relax your jaw, tense with the frustration of oaths unsaid, and open it wide in preparation for clamping down on the object of your desire. Raise your feet, weary from the thud on asphalt roads and feel them light and uncluttered, trailing behind you in cool waters. If you are driving, arch your back, stiff from the concentrated curl around a wheel and imagine that a set of wings has swept you up in the sweet suspense of courtship over a deep green pool. Dream of dragonflies — the original flying dragons with bulbous eyes, aquiline bodies and gargantuan jaws. Dragonfly dreams are summer dreams: rich, ancient and sensuous.

I had a dragonfly dream this week. I was stuck on a hot tin bus travelling along No. 2 Road in Richmond, Vancouver — now a "Poormond" of dragonflies. I had momentarily closed my eyes to shut out the malls and hot car roofs when suddenly I was transformed into a stunning damselfly flying around a No. 1

wetland. I had emerged out of a cool swamp into the lazy heat of that kind of day when the sap of the cattails and bulrushes runs down the leaves and into your brain. There I was, a teneral or emergent nymph, tenderly unfolding my new wings as I clung to a sedge, with a hidden view of dragonfly life that has few rivals.

Dragonfly dreamers should know that there are three families of dragonflies: damselflies, jewelwings and dragonflies. Damselflies and jewelwings are the daintier, small ones that go by such poetic names as Emerald Spreadwing (*Lestes dryas*). Dragonflies are typically larger and appear more prosaic. Dragonfly watchers lump them into groups with names that suggest their behaviour, such as darners (*Aeschnidae*), skimmers and meadowhawks (*Libellulidae*).

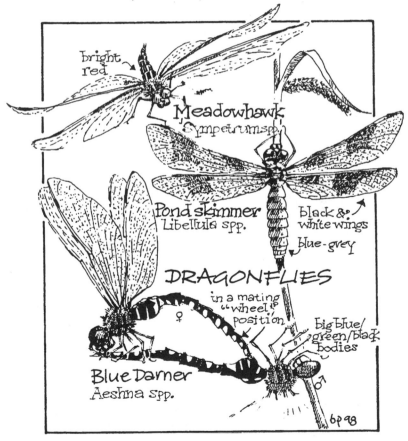

bright red

Meadowhawk
Sympetrum spp.

Pond skimmer
Libellula spp.

black & white wings
blue-grey

DRAGONFLIES

in a mating "wheel" position

big blue/ green/black bodies

Blue Darner
Aeshna spp.

bp 98

Dragonfly behaviour is all about courtship. There are two strategies for courtship: patrolling and perching. Patrollers, such as the darners (the common big black-and-blue or green dragonflies) work the edges of the water, poking in and out of the reeds in search of coy females. The perchers, such as the brilliant red meadowhawks and black-and-white-winged skimmers, stake out territory and then wait for a female or prey to fly into it. If another male flies in, then they have a skirmish and the victor wins the perch.

As far as dreams go, there is nothing like the arrival of a male meadowhawk. All four wings are moving independently to manoeuvre his stunning scarlet body as close to a female as quickly as possible. His speed is colossal, his controlled stops exquisite. Then, with delicate claspers at the end of his abdomen, he grasps his lover's body by the head and carries her away. At this stage in my dream, the dinger on the bus went and I was suddenly back at the Richmond Exchange — which once might have signified an important event for the mating dragonfly couple but now is a rather tedious place to change buses.

The next bus ride was bound for the ferry and there was a better chance to see real dragonflies but after a few miles of more wetlands drained for malls, my eyelids drooped again and I was back in the land of the meadowhawks. All around me, females were swinging by their heads through the cattails, using the opportunity to check out their mates. Some males had grabbed the wrong species and wound up with unresponsive females. But those females who found favour with their mate swung their abdomens up to the base of the male's abdomen, allowing the transfer of sperm. Bus transfers will never be the same.

In my dream, one successful pair circled around until the female released her eggs into the water and the next generation floated gently down to the bottom — a life cycle 300,000,000 years old. Meanwhile, as a slowly maturing damselfly, I had two weeks of leisure to watch my generation, a year or more on from the egg stage, emerge from the water. Larvae, like their adult phase, have evolved different strategies for survival: climbers fight for positions on the rushes; sprawlers lounge around in the mud; and burrowers find themselves a dark hole. I was a social climber.

The bus was jolting along at rush hour and dragonfly dreams and reality merged rather seamlessly at times. The driver's speed was not colossal and his controlled stops less than exquisite. Members of the next generation, who had floated gently to the bottom, packed the bus and I had to grasp my head with my pincers and remove it from the adjacent seat.

My dream came to a close as the sea air blew in through the doors. My wings had finally hardened off and I had been ready to fly to a suitable marsh. My eyes had been shining — all thousand of them — in anticipation of a nuptial flight, when the bus pulled in at the passenger terminal. The passage from a magical marsh full of flying dragons to a black-top terminal full of trucks was rude and abrupt. I waved to the driver in his blue darner uniform (he was a percher) and departed on my weary feet for Berth No. 3. Berth No. 3, Road No. 2 — these are places that drive one to dream. Dream that one day we will leave real No. 1 wetlands for flying dragons.

Hypnotized: Harbour Seals Cast a Soothing Spell

Hypnosis is a method of causing people to enter a sleeplike state during which, through the power of suggestion, they might do remarkable, foolish or embarrassing things. There are two hypnotic states: deep and light. The entire world is currently under a light hypnotic state, induced by television, during which we do foolish and embarrassing things which aren't all that remarkable. But deep states, during which truly remarkable things can be suggested, are rare. Only one in five people can be put into a deep state. Hypnotists who can induce the deep state come in a range of shapes and sizes, and with differing motives and talent. I don't think they're even confined to the human race. Legend has it that cobras hypnotize their victims. But did you know that seals hypnotize people too?

This theory is based on my husband's testimonial involving a seal. Some people may believe in Sasquatch or *Cadborosaurus* but he believes that a seal hypnotized him, dragged him into the sea and through the power of suggestion caused him to do rather remarkable things. How else could he explain getting married to an environmentalist, having more than one child and trying to paint wildlife for a living?

Seals are perfectly suited for inducing deep hypnosis. The subject must want to be hypnotized and be in a comfortable position in a place that is very quiet; the subject then becomes transfixed by a small light and a dull, monotonous tone. The classic type of encounter with a seal is out in a small boat drifting around kelp beds in a peaceful bay. You are usually out there to empty your mind of the details and are actively seeking a hypnotic state. The water is calm and dark. The surface gently breaks and two large and lustrous eyes rise out of the water. As

1.6 m

Our only resident seal that breeds throughout its range. diet is mostly small fish

Silkies are seals that can turn themselves into humans.

HARBOUR SEAL
Phoca vitulina

Vulnerable times for seals are when they are raising their young from July to September you lie there, slumped over the gunwales, you stare at those eyes and the monotonous tone of motorboats throbbing in the distance tells you that you are getting sleepy, sleepy, sleepy ....

Who knows what happens then? When you come out of a deep hypnotic state, you often have no memory of what you did — or with whom you did it. The eyes you were staring at belonged to the Harbour Seal (*Phoca vitulina*), the only resident seal along this coast. Harbour Seals are found in the Atlantic and the Pacific, and everywhere they live, there are stories about them — probably because, for better or for worse, they bump up against human lives. They are highly visible animals, as they always favour quiet places sheltered from winter storms with rocky places to land and bask on during low tide. They are vilified by the fishing industry for their predilection for fish. There was a Canadian bounty on them from 1913 until 1964. Their pelts are luxurious enough that a fur industry thrived until 1969. But something enabled the seals to survive. My theory is that they hypnotized people and enlisted their help.

In Scotland, people told stories about female seals, called "silkies," who could climb up onto the land, take off their fur coats and mate with humans. If the skin of the seal was stolen while it was in human form, the seal could never return to the sea. This certainly points to the possibility that there were some hairy hypnotists swimming around the sea lochs, entrancing the fishermen into keeping furry coats in the closet and having funny babies with webbed toes. Meanwhile on the Pacific, coastal people told stories about seals who mesmerized overzealous seal hunters and dragged them into the ocean for a fitting punishment.

The secret of the seals is their large eyes and pupils. When they are under water, they must be able to dilate their pupils to catch every stray glimmer of light in the darker depths. Their diet for most of the year consists of small sculpins, flatfish and rockfish that glint between the seaweeds. When above water they have to spot the transient Orcas and humans that are their main predators. Their adaptable circular pupils have pin pricks of light at the centre — light at the end of a tunnel which draws you in. In our household, the question will always remain: Was it those eyes that deeply hypnotized my husband to such a state that he flung himself over the edge of the boat, swam into my open flippers and pledged his undying love? He claims that the proof lies in my seemingly unquenchable desire to deliver diatribes against overfishing and jetski boats, and the fact that both our children have webbed toes.

Sometimes he regrets throwing out the furry coat in the closet but the number of seals has certainly climbed back from the old bounty days.

How successful seals will be in surviving the disappearance of quiet places and fish into the next millennium is anyone's guess. I wish somehow the world could tune in one night to the glow of the seals' eyes, instead of television, and through the power of suggestion be induced to do more really remarkable things for the world.

SEX, SWEAT AND SALAMANDERS: HOT HUNT FOR COOL CREATURES

It was the cool, sensitive fingers and sweet smell of honest sweat that first drew me to the type of man who searches for salamanders. Imagine everything you secretly admire about lumberjacks but with a pair of sensitive hands — sensitive enough to feel the infinitesimal rasp of a salamander tooth with a fingertip. And then imagine the kind of man who will go to great lengths to understand a creature that is less understood than Mars. For these reasons, I always get attracted to herpetologists (someone who studies reptiles and amphibians) and can usually be found in the lush lap of an ancient forest in May.

I once spent two dreamy days following around herpetologists who were doing inventories of the more secretive of the *plethodon* or terrestrial salamanders on the coast. To fully appreciate this experience and the qualities of the herpetologist you have to understand a little of the life cycle of these salamanders.

Unlike herpetologists, salamanders have only cool, sensitive toes and don't sweat — they transpire. They breathe through their skin. *Plethodon* means "many toothed" but in fact the more obvious distinguishing feature of these animals is two slender grooves that run between their eyes and their lips: two ritual lines that mark them as land breeders. They don't migrate to swamps and breed in the water like other amphibians. The most common *plethodon* (though common is never a word applied to them) is the Western Redback Salamander, which lives amongst the bark, woody debris and sword ferns in the forests that remain from Vancouver Island to mid-Oregon. After I discovered this, the forest floor has never been the same for me. What I once dismissed as an untidy jumble of wood, I now realize is a kingdom of tunnels, castles and bedrooms to the mighty monarchs of the forest — the flaming redbacks.

To avoid trampling salamanders, herpetologists hover like courtiers but with the stamina of a soldier. Ducking under enormous nurse logs (downed, decayed logs that act as a nursery to young seedlings) and skimming over Skunk Cabbage swamps,

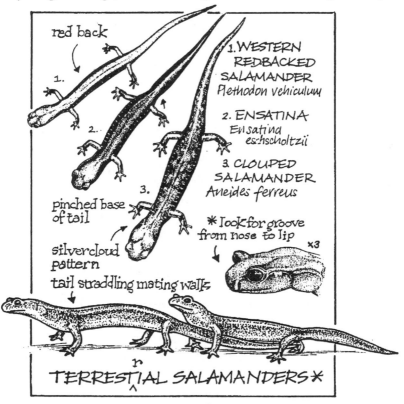

red back

1. WESTERN REDBACKED SALAMANDER
Plethodon vehiculum

2. ENSATINA
Ensatina eschscholtzii

3. CLOUDED SALAMANDER
Aneides ferreus

pinched base of tail

* look for groove from nose to lip ×3

silvercloud pattern

tail straddling mating walk

TERRESTIAL SALAMANDERS *

63

they search the floor on wet days and nights when the salamanders, who spend most of their time underground, come to the
surface to forage and mate. To measure and sex a redback, the
herpetologists must catch and hold the delicate, slippery animal
briefly between cold, confident fingers and run their index finger
under its lip to feel for the male's tiny teeth.

Then there is the Clouded Salamander. The Cloudeds are
found on Vancouver Island and in Oregon but not in
Washington. Named for the silver-like clouds that mottle its
dark, slippery skin, these *plethodon* dwell in the dark heart of
partly decayed logs. They are so light and drought sensitive that
they hardly stray from these small chambers except to mate and
forage. They even lay their eggs there, suspended by small
threads to the ceiling. To find them, herpetologists have developed the strength of a lumberjack and the sensitivity of a
butterfly so they don't destroy the salamanders in the attempt. I
watched my salamander man find one less than six centimetres
(two inches) long in the heart of a huge, fallen tree. This kind of
attention to detail is extremely attractive and what I particularly
liked was that, once he'd found and released the salamander, the
habitat was delicately returned to its original state.

Then there is the widest-ranging *plethodon*, the Ensatina,
monarch of the standing snags, wood piles and rock rubble from
south of the Alaskan panhandle down into Oregon. I watched as
one herpetologist searched fruitlessly through a pile of rocks,
carefully turning over every stone and returning it exactly as it
was found. Undeterred, he chanced to look into a nearby pool
where he saw a desperate clawing of water by a pale Ensatina
pinned under by a Roughskin Newt (a salamander which has an
aquatic breeding phase). He reached into the water and gently
pried the drowning female Ensatina from the clutches of the
male newt. The newt had obviously got confused and dragged
the wrong species into the pool to mate with. A herpetologist
would never do that.

If we had been in southern Washington or Oregon, we would
have looked for a few more rare and isolated species of salamanders — as rare as old-growth forest. For most of them, very little
is known. Consider that only one nest has ever been docu-

mented for the largest *plethodon*, Dunn's Salamander, deep in a rock crevice near a forested stream.

And so the inventory continued and I found myself ready to follow my herpetologists into any lush rainforest they pointed at. Herpetologists do inventories for three reasons. The first two reasons are official. The first is to learn more about them. From what scientists have gathered so far, salamanders eat small organisms which few other species can, making them fundamental links in the forest food web.

The second reason is to determine what happens to these creatures when forest cover is removed. As a class of vertebrates, they are disappearing very quickly from the earth, probably from a combination of factors brought on by habitat loss and climatic change. What will happen to forest ecosystems and ourselves if they disappear? In one study, a herpetologist determined the total weight of all the salamanders in a section of forest and compared it to the total weight of other predators in the same section, such as cougars. Salamanders might be small but they are top predator by collective weight.

The final reason is that this is sexy work. We need sexy work again. Now that lumberjacks have been reduced to a handful of inert machine operators who never catch a whiff of cedar, miners have taken up stockbrokering and fishermen only catch the odd shiner off the dock, there are no jobs with honest outdoor sweat any more. Some may claim hockey players as the last bastion of sex appeal. I say a pair of thick mitts in a cold rink will never compete with those sensitive fingers in a lush and verdant rainforest.

BAGGING A SEA OTTER: UNLEASHING A KELP

In 1533, an act was passed in England that demanded that the church wardens pay a bounty for every corpse of a River Otter and other "vermin" brought in by parishioners. If you browse through the church records, you can count how many corpses were brought in each year before the act was abolished at the turn of the 20th century. It's dreary reading. Life seemed to plod along between surviving birth, bagging an otter, not keeping up with your church tithes, marrying a few months before your first child was born and dying. You shuffled off to church dragging your otter behind you, then thanked God for "all creatures great and small."

When there were no otters left to catch, you could emigrate to the colonies along the northwest coast to assist in exterminating the Sea Otters along the Pacific coast. The significance today of this 400-year-old tradition is that for the last two generations there's been a bit of a change in attitude as regards otters. With the new millennium, we are celebrating the fact that the Sea Otter has been shifted from the endangered list to the threatened, and that bagging an otter has come to mean a completely different thing.

The Sea Otter became extinct in British Columbia in 1929; the last one was shot in Kyuquot Sound on the west coast of Vancouver Island to prove the fact. One remnant population survived in Alaska and another in California. Between 1969 and 1972, 89 Sea Otters were reintroduced to Kyuquot from Alaska and numbers have increased to over 1,500 today along the west coast of Vancouver Island. The only thing that hasn't changed in our mindsets is the confusion over the names of otters. There are two species of otters on the coast but many people think our common River Otter is the Sea Otter. For your reference, use this rule of thumb — if in doubt, it's a River Otter.

The otter you see everywhere along the shore, rivers and lakes of the island is the River Otter. It is slightly larger than a big cat and slips in and out of the water along the shoreline from Oregon to Alaska. It does not crack sea urchins on its stomach with rocks — that's the Sea Otter. The Sea Otter is the size of a small adult human and spends all of its life in the wild, woolly waters of the northwest coast, tangled amongst the kelp and surf. To witness the Sea Otter you have to take a rough ocean voyage for the privilege — hence the new meaning of bagging an otter is to actually see one and capture it on film.

I bagged my first Sea Otter from a pirate ship a few years ago. I was so keen to adapt my ancestral inclinations toward otters that we found a rock-bottom charter outfit consisting of a captain who could teach Captain Bligh a few things and a boat that looked as if it had never been retired from the otter-pelt trade. When I aimed my camera from the heaving, sea-washed deck, I realized that the otter population hadn't entirely erased, from their collective memory, bad associations with humans pointing cylindrical objects at them. The upper torso of one of these richly furred animals was momentarily frozen above the frothy surf before quickly sinking into the blue. It descended the 40 or so metres to its supply of Purple Sea Urchins and Northern Abalones, and freedom from inquisitive humans.

My photograph is a testimony to modern otter bagging and all amateur wildlife photography. It's dreary viewing. The otter head is indistinguishable from the kelp heads to which its life and young are attached. The most interesting thing about the picture is the kelp — the quantity of it. In the 40 years between the extinction and reintroduction of Sea Otters, kelp forests had virtually disappeared due to the appetite of hungry sea urchins

1.6 metres
(1 billion hairs)

present range

SEA OTTERS

Enhydra lutris

largest member of the musteid or weasel family

unchecked by their main predator, the otter. With the return of the Sea Otter, the kelp forests have reestablished themselves, along with many other fish and invertebrates which rely upon the habitat.

Research into the Sea Otters and kelp forests has been going on wherever they have been reintroduced: monitoring the population and the relationship of Sea Otters to their marine habitat; documenting their expansion back into their traditional range; keeping an eye on potential threats like oil spills; watching the impact of kayaking and natural-history tours in the area. What researchers say is that the risk to otters is still very real. Oil spills are always a threat and in places where Orcas are losing traditional food sources, Sea Otters are becoming targets. As tourists, we put our own pressures on them: we should allow 100 metres between ourselves and any individual and let them know we are there.

My advice is don't hire dubious sea captains with no eco-tour guide certification, leave your camera behind and buy postcards instead. Then, when you shuffle off to your spiritual places, dragging your otter postcards behind, you'll be able to show people exactly what these wonderful creatures great and small really look like.

June

How Not to Travel in June:
Flesh-eating Crabs and Fatal Outhouses

Literary humpbacks and albatross. Jeeps and giants in Cathedral Grove. Solstice with crabs in a rowboat. Earthquakes without goldfinches. These are a few of the ideas I jotted down in my journal one June as I did a bit of roaming in search of inspiration. Travel writing, I am told, is a difficult genre to break into. Here are a few tips on how not to travel.

June 1st, Gwaii Haanas.

Many days in wet-weather gear have left the entire crew wrinkled. Today dawned clear and warm though. Everyone is full of anticipation for seeing exceptional things after the rain — such as the sun, our skin, albatrosses and humpbacks. We discovered last night that if you read aloud a story or a poem about a particular thing that you would like to see, it appears.

It all started with the skipper's ditty about puffins and Michael the Haida Watchman's story about ravens. There was nothing but puffins (both Tufted and the rarer Horned species) and Common Ravens for hours afterwards. So I started madly reading

The Ryme of the Ancient Mariner to invoke an albatross. Half way through "water water everywhere" — which caused a bit of alarm with some of the crew — a Laysan's Albatross flew into sight and wheeled like a huge balsa plane over the bow of the boat. I was so excited that we reached for *Moby Dick* and sure enough, a lone Humpback Whale surfaced just to port, its hump breaking the surface with hardly a ripple. A mad dash to the ship's library was made by all, and literature, ranging from *Gone with the Wind* to *The Flight of the Iguana*, was read very loudly from the deck of the

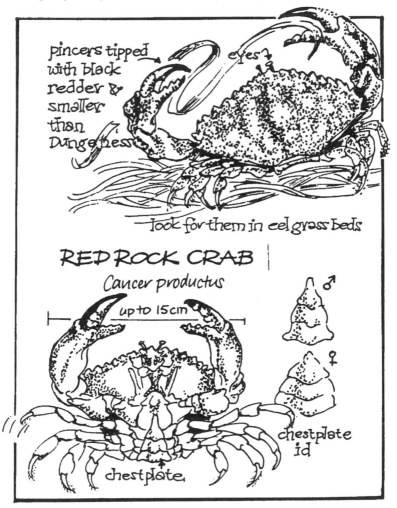

pincers tipped with black redder & smaller than Dungeness

eyes?

look for them in eel grass beds

RED ROCK CRAB
Cancer productus

up to 15cm

♂

♀

chestplate id

chestplate

boat. Since we had insufficient seriousness and solemnity to befit the occasion, neither Clark Gable nor an iguana appeared, but the essence of the day remained as vivid as the sky above us.

June 10th, Cathedral Grove.

It was late. Drove by Cathedral Grove, Vancouver Island's tribute to confusing and malleable metaphors. It was raining. The whole dripping forest was illuminated by pulsing strobes. The Jeep Corporation was filming a commercial showing that even a downed, 1,000-year-old, ten-foot-diameter Douglas-fir in the middle of the night can't stop a good 4x4. Maybe they will leave a jeep hanging from its winch off a moss-laden branch to provide another ambiguous symbol in the park for us to ponder over. "Are corporate sponsors bailing out the environment or should they be hung?" We already have the confused metaphors of the big trees. "We're lucky that the timber barons had the vision to leave us a patch" or "How sad the rest has all gone." Then there are the fallen giants from La Niña's winter storm. "Ancient trees are meant to fall down anyway," versus "Maybe we have created an unstable island in a sea of clearcuts."

But my favourite park symbol is now the women's outhouse. Right after some winter blowdowns, I was clambering over the eerie aftermath when I decided to pay a visit to the Ladies. A branch had pierced the outhouse in such a way that you would only have survived the event, without being impaled, if you remained sitting on the pot with your head down. One could take this as a metaphor of a warning to goddesses in the harsh, corporate, anti-environmental backlash or nature's tip on how to survive.

June 21st, Midsummer's Night. A beach on an island in the Salish Sea.

Midsummers, a group of us assemble on a beach for a solstice and full moon party. Bachanalians rarely consult tide charts because we live to eat, drink and be merry and all that. The tide rose until ten o'clock and the picnic rose just a few inches ahead of it. The party finally had to be moved into a rowboat and we stood around it, in one foot of water, waiting for the sun and tide to go down and the moon to come up. Children were floating away on pieces of driftwood, and we still did not abandon our program. What eventually broke up the party was the crabs.

Red Rock Crabs and the rarer Dungeness were moving into the section of the beach that had not been foraged since the last plus tide and the salmon picnic and ice-chilled toes provided more substance to the bounty. Collected to death in the Salish Sea, it's payback time for these lovely crabs. As the sun set, we escaped into the small rowboat, packed in like a can of sardines, and chanted songs about predatory seagulls. We should have turned to *Midsummer Night's Dream* — "Lord what fools these mortals be."

June 25th, Crofton, a pulp-mill town on Vancouver Island.

There are those who are prepared for earthquakes and those who aren't. As I have demonstrated with my disregard of tides, I fall into the latter. I met one of the prepared sort today. I was stuck at the side of the road somewhere near Crofton. I had a flat bike tire and I didn't have my pump (there seems to be a pattern here). I was singing "Oh Lord, won't you buy me a Mercedes Benz" when a big truck stopped. It was filled to the brim with devices for emergencies, and a man prepared for any of them. The pump he produced ran off the cigarette lighter. He even had an ozonator for making stagnant ditches drinkable should he be caught out on the road during an emergency. He had every statistic on earthquakes ever recorded and a video on every earthquake ever filmed. He was full of chat about a recent earthquake and intent on predicting when the big one was going to hit.

I offered my observations on goldfinches and earthquakes. Any time I have experienced an earthquake, the bird chorus has gone quiet just prior to it. The morning chorus — Purple Finches, American Goldfinches, Swainson's Thrushes and Spotted Towhees — would go quiet with precisely one minute to anticipate the quake. Having never before considered any member of the animal kingdom as anything but a post-emergency food supply, the truck driver was most interested in my observations. I suspect he will become an avid watcher of birds as well as earthquake videos. And maybe I will begin to carry pumps, tide tables and a flask of freshwater — and will remember to keep my head down when I sit on the pot.

ENRAPTURED BY RAPTORS

Raptures. It is a new party trend, hot off the thermals, where everyone gets rapturous. To get high you just flap your arms. The music is kind of different too. It's all vocalizations, with variable wing beats, and neighbours don't object. Instead of a big crowd, the party can get off the ground with only nine guests. You have to dress up. You pick one of the nine raptors or birds of prey *(rapt* is Latin for "to seize hold of") that hang out on the coast and you take on their persona for the night. Out of the nine, there is a bird to suit every personality.

You might choose the Bald Eagle persona. Bald Eagles are reflective types. They are so big and require so much energy to fly around that they measure the odds for success before entering into any activity, whether it is looking for a mate or prey, or deciding where to build their nest. They are the dependable, solid type but not very innovative or spontaneous. Love fish, especially ones that have been conveniently caught for them or are dying on the beach. They'll chase after the odd duck when the salmon aren't around. Can be a bit of a thug to other raptors that come into their space. Rather dapper though, with a white head, white tail and dark suit.

The Red-tailed Hawk is good for a flamboyant mood when you want to dress up with a big red fan-shaped tail and soar around the party in wide circles looking for cute rodents. Red-tailed aren't as big as eagles, wings are smaller and chunkier but they cover more territory. Spend most of their time flying and making long plaintive cries, which has a lot to commend it at a party.

The Turkey Vulture is a great one to explore your alter ego. You wear an all-black costume except for a bright red, tiny, naked head. Puts off all advances except other Turkey Vultures exploring their alter ego. Easy to spot because they fly like a kite — kind of V-shaped with a bit of a rock and roll to it. Soar most of the time, circling down from the highs to check out the odd dead snake or rodent. The strong, silent, ugly, Phantom-of-the-Opera type. Head south in the winter.

The Osprey is for the sophisticated jocks of the group. They have these gorgeous white thighs that can really turn an eye. They can be put to good use, too. One minute they are discreetly tucked up under their striped tail, then the next minute, they are thrusting down into the water to scoop up a hefty, five-kilo salmon. Flashy bird for the latent extrovert and you get to dress up in a black jacket with a white shirt and trousers, sporting a sexy little silver streak in your hair. One of the few that get to hover at the party.

For the spontaneous opportunists there are two bird hawks: Cooper's Hawk and Sharp-shinned. Because they hunt other birds among the trees they have a sort of furtive, swoop-and-kill approach. They are quite an exciting duo. They both have rusty barred breasts and long stripey tails but stubby, barred underwings for negotiating the understory. The Cooper's is bigger and has a rounder tail than the Sharp-shinned, which is not much use for identification unless they are together for comparison. Try both.

For the slick, sleek and slender, hit-'em-out-of-nowhere types, there are three falcons in descending order of size: Peregrine Falcon, Merlin and American Kestrel. These raptors are bird hunters in open country so their chief quality is speed and they are built for it. If you are lucky enough to see a Peregrine Falcon at an eyrie you might get a glimpse of it pulling the head off some victim and telling the world about it. Otherwise, it is a hurtling dart in the sky. You could have fun with the outfit as it is silver sequins on the front, black curls and dark cape. Peregrines are reinhabiting cities because of the pigeons, so an eyrie might be a penthouse suite. If it is a small blur, then it is a Merlin. The Kestrel, on the other hand, hovers and is a colourful combination of red head and tail, black moustaches, blue-grey wings and polka-dot trousers. Kestrels are a bit bigger than a swallow and occasionally hang out around road kills.

There is one unwritten code at a raptor party. You have to maintain territory. This leads to interesting encounters. With everyone soaring, diving or hovering around at different levels of the sky, there is an obvious order or niche into which one could fit. If you are not doing very well in one niche and find you are getting thugged up by an eagle one too many times, you might want to change costume. Come back as a Kestrel and unobtrusively hover.

It doesn't take long to learn their basic habitats and behaviour. The real fun comes in learning the subtle details of their lives and how they hold territory. In fact, soon you will find yourselves scanning the sky at every opportunity to witness them first hand. You might become obsessive and start erecting plucking posts (stumps where they pluck their victims to eat them) and planting future old-growth trees in your backyard for them to build nests in. You'll start reintroducing voles into city parks and salmon into city creeks. You'll vote for councillors who want to protect their nests. You'll stand up and be counted for the Endangered Species Act. You'll defend the preservation of habitat to the end and collapse in ecstatic rapture as twilight falls.

CLAMS FOR RUBY

If you have a room full of unruly kids, threaten them with this exercise. Gather a pile of burlap sacks and ask the biggest ones to curl up on a sack, then lay sacks on top of them. Get the next biggest ones to lie on top of them and put sacks over them. Then get the littlest to lie on top of them and put the final sacks over the whole lot. While everyone is suffocating under burlap, hand out straws and suggest they poke the straws or siphons up to the surface for air. Tell them that they are now clams and to think about the lives of the following clams.

The biggest ones at the bottom are Horse Clams — irregular-shaped shells, as big as an outstretched palm, with long, tough, sinewy siphons. The middle ones are Butter Clams — oval, yellow to grey-white in colour and as big as a closed palm. The little ones at the top are Little-necks — oval, as long as the middle finger, patterned with radiating stripes and a little siphon. The sacks represent sand and this is how the clams live in the sand. If you have endured this mild form of torture as a child you will never forget clam species order in the protected intertidal sandflats of the Salish Sea. Ruby Alton, my neighbour, said so and she was nearly 70 when she told me.

When Ruby's schoolteacher was dealing with unruly children and burlap sacks, it was the Depression and this information was critical to a schoolgirl's education. Clams supplemented the diet and could be sold for extra money to stretch the family income. Knowing species was important, as there were different rates for different species. Times have changed. The teachers probably couldn't get away with packing boys and girls between sacks to demonstrate clam behaviour. Clams are not on the curriculum any more.

I think about Ruby's story whenever I walk the beach below her forest that she has left as a sanctuary. The creek that runs through the forest and out to the sea has created a wonderfully gravelly, muddy place for clams. These three species were the ones she talked about and dug for when I joined her on clam-digging expeditions there. We went down with one bucket and a spade, her hair wrapped up in a bright kerchief. She dug, I gathered. She told me she was always a Little-neck — the advantage of being a smaller girl. Her brothers were Horse Clams. They were the toughest and least tasty. We laughed because we

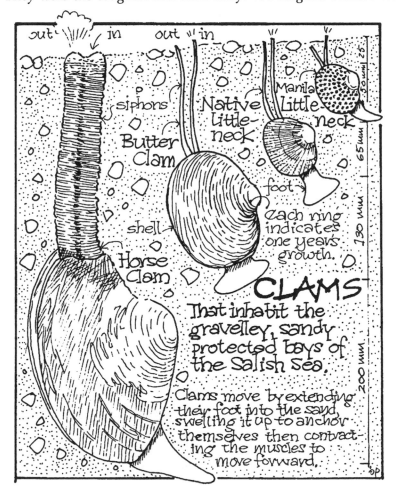

out • in   out • in

siphons

Manila Little-neck

Native Little-neck

Butter Clam

30 mm

65 mm

130 mm

foot

each ring indicates one year's growth.

shell

Horse Clam

CLAMS
That inhabit the gravelley, sandy protected bays of the Salish Sea.

Clams move by extending their foot into the sand, swelling it up to anchor themselves then contracting the muscles to move forward.

200 mm

both had lots of big tough brothers who deserved to be at the bottom of the sacks. Butter Clams were the plumpest and the best tasting, she said. We laughed because we are both skinny, bony women never destined for refined luxury palates.

To dig for a Horse Clam you have to go down at least a foot into the mud. Those large squirts that you get in embarrassing places when you tread across the mud are the Horse Clam siphons retreating into their shells. They can be quite a tussle to get. The Butter Clams only need an eight-inch probe with a sharp spade, and Ruby could flick out Little-necks with a fierce glare. It was probably her kerchief. The Little-necks she dug for as a schoolgirl were now joined by an introduced species called the Manila Little-neck which have geometric patterns, are shinier and more oblong, and even closer to the surface than the native Little-necks. I knew she had somewhat less respect for the newcomers as they were less tolerant of extreme winters, being so close to the surface, although to her pragmatic eye any food was a gift.

Horse Clams live to be quite old, she reckoned, as long as a person although not as long as Geoducks ("gooeyduck" is a native Nisqually word for "dig deep" because these clams live way down in the sand) which can live up to 150 years. She didn't have Geoducks on her beach, otherwise her teacher would have put a few of them down at the bottom for another sack layer. Butter Clams live about 20 years and Little-necks are shortlived, being close to the surface. You have to take more of the ebbs and flows of life up at the top; that is the disadvantage of being a Little-neck.

Ruby lived and died a Little-neck. She stuck her little neck out to face the ebbs and flows of the 20th century. She knew what she was talking about when she saw the ability to feed yourself in the Salish Sea disappear due to overfishing, habitat loss and pollution. She knew what would happen when you dropped clams from the curriculum. Before she died she told me she hoped these places and species would hang on. So Ruby, here is one of your stories, and when your ashes find their way down that creek into the estuary, I'll look for that Little-neck with the bright kerchief.

WOODPECKERS AND MALE DRUMMING

The world might have seen more spectacular film sets than a snag by our sandbox, but few could argue that the main actor wasn't a star. Right on cue, he swooped onto the old dead fir — a flying Thespian with blazing scarlet head, flashing white sideburns and jet black suit — and drummed out a beat on the trunk that stirred every male within a kilometre. The Pileated Woodpecker was starring in a film on the temperate rainforest. The filmmaker was at our snag to film "primary cavity nesters" (the term to describe the animals that excavate their own nests in old or dead trees). Stunned into silence in the sandbox below was one of my own little human primary cavity nesters. He did admirably as supporting actor, convincing us all that forests are places where woodpeckers, old snags and little boys are naturally bonded. As well as having his first male bonding at the age of two with a woodpecker, he experienced another of life's oxymorons — dead trees are the life of the forest.

If you doubt the truth of this statement, go out into the forest and see for yourself. It is not difficult around this time of year to spot a woodpecker; they are all out in force, drumming (tapping on resonant trunks to establish territory), calling, nesting and feeding their young. There are seven different species of woodpeckers on the coast and some of these can be found even in cities, drumming away on the telephone poles. In the forest around my house, I have difficulty hearing the tap tap tap of my keyboard over the din of our resident woodpeckers. The guy who wrote *Still Life with Woodpecker* was either deaf or overstepping his poetic licence.

The best place to listen for woodpeckers is in dead standing trees or what we now call "wildlife trees." The foresters used to call them "decadent snags" (now the term just describes a certain type of emancipated, sensitive New Age guy). Wildlife trees have finally received the attention they deserve. Deep within the rotting humus of these trees lie the clues to the ecology of a forest. There are so many fungi, insects, plants and larger animals which rely on this stage of the tree's life that scientists haven't even begun to identify them all. What they have identified is that woodpeckers are a key link in the lives of most forest species.

What drives woodpeckers to drill weakened trees is the possibility of food and shelter. Overcoming deafness and poetic licence, they create cavities to open the tree up further to fungi and bacteria. The tree then becomes a virtual ark. Nuthatches, owls, squirrels, martens, raccoons and bats — you name it, they rely on old Woody Woodpecker to open up the holes for their nests. They are called "secondary cavity nesters." Cartoonists and kids have known this for years, but not in so many words. Now we need serious documentaries to demonstrate that a forest is a place that includes decadent snags, woodpeckers, kids and bats, not just endless rows of young, genetically improved, super-fibre specimens that are about as flexible as a chainsaw to the whims of nature. You don't have to see the film to have this point demonstrated; simply go outside, find yourself an old rotting tree and catch the action.

Woodpecker watching is a great spectator sport even without a two year old to put out as bait. Start with the Northern Flickers. They are dead easy to spot since they flicker when they fly and flicker when they call. Their red (sometimes yellow) underwings flash during their erratic flight (most woodpeckers have a very distinctive flight: they flap hard for a few seconds to gain elevation, then soar and rapidly lose the height they gained — sort of like movie stars). You might have seen flickers at a feed table in the winter or scouring the ground looking for insects. They are about the size of a ruler, have a black bib and call (flicker, flicker) like an exotic bird that you might hear whilst punting along the Amazon. (Their calls were used in Tarzan movies along with the Pacific Treefrog chorus.) Look in old trees for holes facing north with small heads poking out. I have one by my house and the babies are there this time of year, looking for grub and throwing themselves off from great heights. That much they have in common with my children.

The Pileated Woodpecker, the elusive but spectacular king of woodpeckers, is the archetypical Woody Woodpecker. Their heads pound old trunks and telephone poles with an effect like a

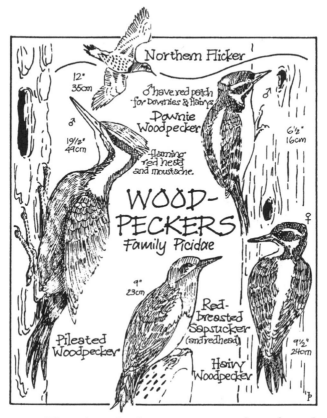

jackhammer. These large birds are uncommon but where there are stands that include quietly rotting trees, there is a good chance of spotting one. They are quite decadent snags themselves.

The two most common little woodpeckers around, with striped black and white wings, are the Downy and the Hairy Woodpecker, neither of which is particularly hairy or downy. They are hard to tell apart unless you see them together, in which case the Hairy is bigger. The males of both species have red patches on the backs of their heads. The Downy is the one you are most likely to see around suburban woods. They love to eat many of our "pests" so they are to be encouraged in every garden. Just in case you see one that looks like these two but has yellow on the back of its head, you have spotted the less common, Three-toed Woodpecker which for the record has three toes.

81

The Red-breasted Sapsucker also lives up to its name. It is red-breasted (and red-headed) and sucks sap from live trees. The sap then attracts insects which they pick up for dessert. You can tell if you have a sapsucker in your wood by the parallel rows of small holes. It looks as if Al Capone has machine gunned the tree. They fledge their young in front of my window which is hell on deadlines. You can also see them drilling dead trees for insects, then they turn their head to listen before resuming their drilling. I think they are listening for the cries of impending doom from the bug in the sap. Someone described my writing with the same words so I have empathy for the bug.

Finally, there is the Lewis' Woodpecker which only makes rare guest appearances. I have only ever seen one, dancing for flies from a large old snag (it's a hard word to shake). It is a nine-inch-tall, red-faced, white-breasted and green-backed bird which actually prefers to catch insects on the wing. Its habitat is open, natural savannahs like Garry Oak meadows which are almost as rare as this bird.

The best time to enjoy woodpeckers is before the height of summer when they all disappear into the woodwork. Find an old tree and bond with your decadent snag or his progeny to the beat of the drums.

TENT CATERPILLARS:
GULLIVER'S TRAVELS TO BROBDINGNAG

I was reading *Gulliver's Travels* to some Lilliputians the other day and discovered to my amazement that on the 16th day of June, 1703, Gulliver got swept up in a storm and ended up on a great island somewhere between southeast Alaska and Vancouver Island. Gulliver describes the country as being bounded on the northeast by volcanoes and surrounded by lots of rough seas. The island — Brobdingnag — is inhabited by 600,000 giants who are as tall as church steeples and knock the odd whale off to feed themselves.

The tale was certainly close enough to home to elicit further interest. The story goes that Gulliver is rescued by a kind giantess, learns the language and eventually ends up with the giant king, telling him all about the society from which he comes. Gulliver discusses the European justice system, the structure of institutions, the distribution of wealth and the control of resources. Then he tries to explain how the invention of gunpowder has monopolized the control of all these noble institutions, wealth and resources. After a great deal of questioning, the king responds by telling him that his society must be the most "pernicious race of little odious vermin that nature ever suffered to crawl upon the surface of the earth."

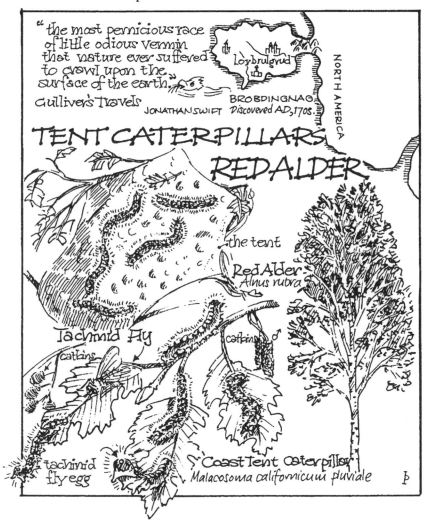

"the most pernicious race of little odious vermin that nature ever suffered to crawl upon the surface of the earth."

Gulliver's Travels
JONATHAN SWIFT

Loybrulgrud

BROBDINGNAG
Discovered AD, 1705.

NORTH AMERICA

TENT CATERPILLARS
RED ALDER

the tent

Red Alder
Alnus rubra

Tachinid Fly
catkins

catkins

tachinid
fly egg

Coast Tent Caterpillar
Malacosoma californicum pluviale

As we were sitting out under the Red Alder trees, agreeing heartily with Jonathan Swift's famous allegory, 25 tent caterpillars fell onto my head, arms, book, lap, mouth and legs. These stalwart larvae were duly rescued lovingly by the small people, placed in yoghurt containers and observed intently (no pun intended). Only just resisting the urge to crunch them all under my feet, I found myself wanting to declare, like the giant king, that these were the most pernicious race of little odious vermin that nature has ever suffered to crawl upon the surface of the earth. But thanks to Swift's biting satire and clarity of vision, it was apparent that there was some irony here and cause for questioning the status quo on attitudes to tent caterpillars.

One small person pointed out that, relative to the giants of Brobdingnag, Gulliver is about the same size as a tent caterpillar. I, the giantess, was then forced to confront my deepest fears concerning my relationship with nature. This is the time of year when these fears come to the surface. We are forced to either declare war against nature, surrender, or have deeply inconsistent ideas about which species we want to subjugate. I am of the deeply inconsistent variety with selective wars against both introduced species, like broom, ivy, starlings and thistles, and native but ugly species like the Pacific Coast Tent Caterpillars. It is only when you have an audience of Lilliputians who ask uncomfortable questions that you confront your inconsistencies.

It was time to reexamine my feelings for tent caterpillars anyway, because so many people with whom I share no other views share a dislike of this species. It was also impossible to ignore their presence during a bumper tent caterpillar year when they became one of the most visible life forms that we have on the coast. Every seven or so years the population builds up to provide a massive display on our alders, willows, Ocean-spray, and cultivated trees and shrubs. Not the least of their qualities is their ability to awaken an interest in natural history amongst small people with yoghurt containers who love to observe their intricate life cycle, from egg to wriggling black dots on silky tents to hairy caterpillars to pupae to brown moth and back to egg.

It was one such Lilliputian under the alder who focussed my attention on the white dot phenomenon and the path to humility. I'll share this observation. In your wandering through any leafy areas infested with our indigenous coast tent caterpillars, take time to pause, pluck an adult caterpillar off a leaf and check if there is a tiny white dot on its forehead. If the dot is there then rest assured that that caterpillar is a marked individual not long for this world, shortly to be consumed by ravaging maggots of the Tachinid Fly which will devour its internal organs when the caterpillar goes into its cocoon.

Upon having this phenomenon pointed out to me, I was overcome with a sense of great freedom — freedom from the bondage of wanting control over one more species. Instead of wrestling with the frenzied urge to grab every leprous branch festooned with the silk tents of the caterpillar and fling them on a burning pyre, I felt no such compulsion. An inner peace descended because I knew something else, larger or smaller than me, was in control. I had only to replace the doomed larvae upon the branch, allow the Tachinid Fly population to thrive, providing the future checks to the caterpillar cycle, and walk gently about my own business.

A second observation was also made under that alder that lent significance to the role of the humble caterpillar. The alder was an old one with largely dead branches at the top and luxuriant new growth below (being eaten by the caterpillars). A sapsucker nested in the dead portion. Then I realized with great clarity that the reason it was dead at the top was because the tent caterpillars had ravaged the tree several years earlier during their last cycle, and their efforts enabled the sapsuckers to have a home.

I am still inconsistent, especially with regard to my own species. I cannot resist the urge to wish that there was a giant Tachinid Fly that would selectively lay its eggs on multinational corporate executives, but like Gulliver I still have a lot of travels to make.

July

CHASING FEARS AND BATS:
MAYAN GODS TO MOSQUITO KINGS

It all started in a hammock at the point where Guatemala and Belize melt together into the sluggish waters of the Rio Hondo. Bats took over my brain while a tropical fever raged. All I could see from my position was a large vampire bat in the gaping rafters, savouring the evening's blood extracted from a pig that still squealed below me. The bat flitted through my feverish dreams, crossing between death and life, light and darkness, sky and earth. The old verandah that supported my hammock was sliding slowly into the river and I realized I wouldn't be too upset if I joined it.

I got over my fever and the bat flew out of my mind until one month later. In the middle of a monsoonal thunderstorm at Tikal, the ancient Mayan city, I took refuge by huddling in a dark subterranean passage near the Plaza of the Seven Temples. The thin beam of my flashlight danced over an enormous relief sculpted out of the wall. It was the Mayan bat god, Chac, and I was staring my dream bat in the face.

The third time I met him I was deep in a cave surveying Mayan petroglyphs. At night, before we went to sleep a mile under the earth, we would turn off the carbide lamps, our life-

four fingers
thumb

5.5
grams

long-ears protrude
5mm from nose when
pushed

build a
bathouse

WESTERN LONG-EARED
BAT/MYOTIS   *Myotis evotis*

Penn '97

2" max

lines to the world, and the darkness would engulf us completely. The first fretful night I woke in a panic and struck a match. Beside me was a brilliant white pattern on the ground. It was a Mayan offering to the gods — a bat skeleton fossilized in the limestone for an eternal flight.

I am not really scared of the dark any more and I often go on a bit about the virtue of bats — my little messengers between the heavens and the depths of the earth. Even in the familiar light of a summer evening at home, they conjure up romance. I live in a house with a hammock on a faded verandah that is sliding into the sluggish waters of the Rio Fulford and I watch bats all summer evening.

A friend who is a wildlife biologist was checking out the status of bats in this region. She selected my verandah to find out which species we have on our island. Good habitat for bats is anywhere that there are lots of night-flying insects, old trees with crevices to roost in and a wetland nearby. It was a night to remember. It took us two hours to stretch the delicate mist nets across the verandah to block one of their flyways. The principle of the nets is that when bats, who are creatures of routine, get lazy, they will fly their normal path without using their sonar for echolocation and fly straight into the net. Nets set, we all lay in the hammock, boring our kids with bat stories.

By midnight we had seen and heard lots of them but had not caught a single one. The bats were obviously less lazy than our crew, who had fallen asleep. They were feeding busily. This we knew as we had a sonar detector going and could hear their characteristic click click click buzz as they zeroed in on their prey. Bat specialists describe bat sonar as an ability to picture a landscape through sound. A few minutes after midnight, a bat flew into the net. Trained and licensed to handle bats, my friend carefully extracted the small creature with her hands and identified it. This is harder than it sounds. Bats are robust and not afraid when caught. They click and snap at you at an audible level.

As far as identification goes, some of the diagnostic techniques include such instructions as, "Check for minute hairs at the bottom edge of the tail skin," and "Is the hind foot greater or less than 9 mm?" or "Does the calcar have a keel?" Our bat, we think, was the Western Long-eared Myotis, also known as *Myotis evotis*, which sounds like it should be the name of the next secretary-general of the United Nations. We had no difficulty with the diagnostic feature of the male which I can safely say was far longer than his hind foot.

Bats form the most dominant group of small mammals on the coast, with ten different species, in some places more diverse than rodents. The most common bat on the coast (where research has been done) is the Yuma Myotis ("myotis" is a type of bat). Dropping this name into the conversation has been known to impress my friends. If you forget that name you can always fall back on the next two most common bats — the Little Brown Bat (or Myotis) and the Big Brown Bat — inspirational names. Two of the bats on the coast are on the "species at risk" list, Townsend's Big-eared Bat, our only known true hibernating bat, and Keen's Long-eared Myotis which has different ideas about how old growth should be used.

The other five species you might glimpse on the coast are the Long-legged Myotis, California Myotis, Western Long-eared Myotis, Hoary Bat and Silver-haired Bat. The latter two are relatively large and have distinctive salt-and-pepper fur. To positively identify bats requires having a resident bat expert along with nets, sonar detectors and knowledge of bat habitat. Even they can't be assured of telling some of the myotis species apart. Better just to learn the names and chant them in succession as the bats fly by. No one will know you're wrong.

We woke up some of the team to show them a *Myotis evotis* close up — which raised a mixed response. Bats will always raise mixed responses, I suppose. The three misconceptions about bats on the coast are as follows: first, they fly into people's hair; second, they are flying rats; and third, they will bite you and suck your blood or give you rabies. Bats are far better fliers than birds. They use two senses to fly with, sight and hearing, (I have had a bird in my hair but never a bat). Bats, on the evolutionary scale of things, are closer to people than rodents. Vampire bats that suck blood live in the tropics, not here. Rabies is always a concern but you have a greater risk of getting rabies from your pet dog than from a bat.

For pragmatists, bats are important insect controllers. They'll eat 10,000 mosquitoes in a night, and distribute the nutrients from them around the forest. For romantics, they provide good stories and a reason to lie in a hammock with your sweetheart and gaze at the moon.

Is There Life After Nighthawks?: Healing Up High

On the wall of the intensive care unit at our big regional hospital there is a print of a quiet hillside at dusk. It is one of those generic paintings you see in any waiting room where they want to calm you. Wheeling high above the quiet hillside in a sky rising from gold to purple is a small, swallow-like bird. For me the picture doesn't calm; it drives me close to committing acts of vandalism. A few years earlier, had you looked out the hospital window, you would have seen a lovely hillside with scattered oaks, Arbutus and fir. And at dusk, Common Nighthawks swept the sky, as if to reassure you that there was a life to return to after a sickness or loss. Now there is nothing but the results of vandalism, noise and concrete.

Nighthawks can attach themselves to you in a particular way. As birds of dawn and dusk, they come when your thoughts are already lingering on deeper topics than work or meals. And they

gradually wind their way into those thoughts with their melancholy cries that start somewhere around the evening star and glide down into your inner sanctum. The other thing about nighthawks is that you never see them up close. All day they sleep camouflaged in the limbs of the Douglas-firs and Garry Oaks or in their nests on the ground. Their mottled brown plumage is indistinguishable from the leaves, bark and grasses. Come nightfall, they appear way up in the sky — a silhouette of long, pointed wings, forked tail and head with enormous mouth wide open. Back and forth they sweep the sky for insects. I have rarely seen a nighthawk ascend or descend to the ground, a sign that movements between worlds are assured but rarely documented.

While my dad was dying, all we could see out the hospital windows was dust and huge machines. All we could hear were blasts and drilling. While our family sat vigil at his side, the noises continued 24 hours a day. Someone out there wanted to make sure that the new superhighway was ready to take us on a documented journey to a duller world. Where there was once a hill meadow with nighthawk nests, there is now only a suggestion of shrubbery dissected by roads. Sitting in the waiting room, wondering whether my father was going to die that dawn, I needed some reassurance that life returns after loss, but no sounds of nighthawks drifted down from the sky, only the incessant drone of a rock-crushing machine. Someone, I suppose, expected us to close the window, stare at the picture of the quiet hillside at dusk and just imagine the calls of serenity.

My family gathered during this same week a year later for our annual camp-out at a family place under firs and oaks. Out of the blue at midday, a nighthawk cry startled me from a conversation with my brothers and we looked up together. The sky was full of Common Nighthawks circling below the canopy of the forest. They rarely fly so low or during the day. We watched bird after bird join the flock and realized that we were witnessing the start of a mass migration. The white wing patches flashed as they flew between us and the sun. The young ones were indistinguishable from their parents and we could sense the excitement in the air. They circled above our heads for 20 minutes and then were gone, south, spiralling up on a thermal from the change of weather.

There aren't many ways to express to your brothers what you feel when the seasons change, your father dies, or you say goodbye to them for another year. Largely all those things go unsaid. But watching the nighthawks together was just about everything we would have wanted to say. We're thankful that the meadow has remained intact for five generations of our family to hear them. Back at that hospital though, the possibility has gone forever.

I try to imagine dusk without the nighthawks; I know that I can never imitate their call when they have gone. The question is, do we really need to move mountains and quiet hillsides to get better roads and better hospitals? I know one thing: I would rather die a little earlier under the real nighthawks than over a prolonged period in that hospital, staring at a picture, trying to imagine their calls.

HERON AID: GOO-GOO-GOGGLES ON THE BIG BLUE BIRD

What is big, red and eats rocks? What is great, blue and eats fish? Big-Red-Rock-Eater and Great-Blue-Heron. I succumbed. I set out to write an evocative introduction to this beautiful bird and all I could think of was adapting bad riddles from Dr. Seuss. I have a problem with Dr. Seuss; it has taken me years to get beyond the urge to describe the natural world with less than three-hyphenated-adjectives that must rhyme with hat, socks or dish.

With regard to the Great Blue Heron, it is impossible to repress Seuss-like descriptions. They really do look like Swomee-Swans with goo-goo-goggles and four fluffy feathers on a Fiffer-feffer-feff. They commonly roost in colonies in what look like Truffula trees where they build these big-N-little-n-what-begins-with-n Nests and behave like Horton Hatching the Who during the breeding season. No, they do not like green eggs and ham; they eat green frogs and Sam-I-am. Seuss loosely modelled Sam-I-am, I think, on coastal rodents such as the Long-tailed Vole which constitute a major part of their diet.

They also rely on one fish, two fish, red fish, blue fish and prefer to catch these in the rain away from trains, in the dark in a park, along the shore without a roar .... And here I pause, because I can't find anything in Dr. Seuss to rhyme with estuary which is another reason why I dislike his poetry — whole parts of the ecosystem are ignored for their lack of ability to rhyme easily. No wonder this world is in such a mess.

So now you have the general gist of the Great Blue Heron. Most people feel comfortable identifying herons, although my hairdresser always refers to them as cranes — a Great Red Herring. I helpfully told her the Dr. Seuss riddle the other day and now she calls them Great Blue Fisheaters. Whatever you

Heron stretching after a night's fishing

Heron breeding colonies are commonly groves of trees (alder) with large nests located in the crooks of branches — Truffula-tree -like.

Neck pulled in during flight usually

GREAT BLUE HERON
Ardea herodias

Black eyestripe

Fiffer-feffer feff.

130 cm

Crows, ravens & eagles are natural predators of eggs & nestlings.

want to call them, you can see the herons fishing at low tide around estuaries and mudflats in some parts of the Salish Sea. They stand there quietly up to their bellies for hours on one leg, neck coiled like a spring, with their spear-like bill waiting to whack-with-a-sickening-smack the next one-fish-two-fish to swim by. They generally travel two to three kilometres a day from their roosts and breeding colonies (heronries) to good feeding grounds, so you can figure out where to see them from knowing a bit about their heronries, roosts and behaviour.

Our distinctive subspecies of heron on the coast (*Ardea herodias fanninni*), of which there are fewer than 5,000 pairs left, are most likely to be seen around the Salish Sea. Here, the calm waters and rich feeding grounds enable the herons to establish big traditional heronries ("big" can mean over 100 nests) which they inhabit year after year, as well as small, less permanent ones. The bigger traditional heronries, some of which have been recorded over 70 years, include ones in Beacon Hill Park (by Mile 0) in Victoria, Pacific Spirit Park and Stanley Park around Vancouver, Point Roberts on the Fraser delta, Chilliwack, Crofton, Saltspring Island and Nanaimo. There are five large colonies in Washington State. These traditional colonies are relatively stable, although many big ones in the last few years have been abandoned. The small colonies are less permanent but important mixers for the population as a whole.

To see herons in a heronry is better than "a dozen doughnuts and duck dog too," but leave the duck dog behind if you go heron watching. Heron populations are adaptable but only so far. They are now listed as a species at risk. Their feeding grounds are getting more gluppity glupp and schloppity schlop and if the food runs out so do they. The other problem is that the Truffula trees where the smaller colonies roost and breed are being cut down by people who want views for a snooze and lawns for yawns. The herons also have to contend with their traditional enemies — eagles, crows and ravens.

Unusual activity that they are not used to, like a tree being cut down, machinery being operated, a dog barking or even people passing a heronry, can put the parents off the nest and when they leave who comes? Joe comes, Slow Joe Crow comes, after the eggs or nestlings. After one too many crow and eagle attacks, I would probably move on too. This makes it very difficult to officially protect smaller, more temporary heronries (often a grove of cottonwoods or alders), since they might abandon it. Try telling a developer to leave a half-kilometre buffer around a bunch of old alders on the off chance that some Fiffer-feffer-feffs might return to roost there and you might as well expect the Cat in the Hat to come back.

You can see herons elsewhere on the coast in ones and twos. About every 100 kilometres or so of coastline you might run into the odd pair nesting, from the outer coast of Vancouver Island to Prince William Sound. Probably the best chance of seeing herons, though, is on the billboards along coastal highways. Every second marina and RV site from Seattle to Juneau advertises itself with a heron — the one that used to roost or fish there before the marina or RV park was built. The impact of losing these small roosts is not really known, but it is safe to say that the "future is dreary, they'll fly on their wings and get woefully weary" if we don't keep habitat for breeding colonies.

So ... what time is it when the elephant sits on the fence? Time to put Dr. Seuss back in the bookcase, plant a bunch of Truffula alder trees, stop pouring gloppity glopp down your drain and speak out for Fiffer-feffer-feffs.

Moonlight Snailing: Taking the Plunge with Slimy Denizens of Tidal Mud

I have always been very fond of toilet plungers. They remind me of hot summer evenings under a full moon at low tide on the steaming mud sands of the Salish Sea. If you tiptoe out on these mudflats between the slumbering clams and dozing mussels, you might be lucky enough to see a whole landscape of discarded plungers — not the real things, of course, but the egg cases of the Moon Snails that look exactly like the bathroom variety. It gives new meaning to the one that sits in your bathroom when you first witness the natural spectacle of a Moon Snail romancing.

Moon Snails are large sea snails that have turban-shaped shells. The body (technically a "mantle" or foot) is a huge, slimy, amorphous mass that appears much larger than the shell above. You can often see empty Moon Snail shells above the tide line — they are the big ones which collect dust in bathooms. The snails tend to be inconspicuous all winter, lying hidden in the mud out at sea. Come the warmth of the summer months, though, they parade up to the intertidal sands and cavort in crowds.

The outcome of the spring encounters is a flush of plunger-like egg cases. The Moon Snail oozes the eggs out through a cavity round its mantle in a jelly-like sheet. As the gelatinous sheet spreads out, it binds with the sand and forms a perfect collar around the snail. These are what you see at low tide sitting out on the mud, looking like a used dump of bathroom accessories. Later, the egg cases crumble and release millions of little larvae into the ocean.

Having large undisturbed dormitories of mud for slumbering clams and sea snails makes me sleep easy at night. Moon Snails are signs of relatively clean, muddy beaches. Clean mud is the stuff that has a mix of uncontaminated sand and silt in it. On the practical level, it means fresh food. On the ecological level, it is a sign of a functioning marine ecosystem. Moon Snails are voracious predators, a few links up on the food chain from plankton. They plough through the mud eating clams, mussels and any other molluscs or dead flesh in their path. They attack their prey by either drilling a hole into its shell and sucking the flesh out or suffocating it in their massive foot. There is also a strong likelihood that the area has lots of sunflower stars — the Moon Snail's main predator.

Sunflower stars are second only to Moon Snails for having the slimiest, weirdest bodies ever to inspire manufacturers of rubber gadgets. This sea star is reminiscent of something between the Slime Slurp and a Star Wars villain. They are huge, slimy, rapid-moving stars, sometimes reaching a metre across, with as many as 25 legs that are mottled colours of purple, orange and greeny grey — an interior decorator's nightmare. They are also breeding down in the mud right now and you can see all their little darlings getting ready to grow and become the scourges of the mudflats.

Sunflower Star
*Pycnopodia
helianthoides*

sunflower star
attacking a
moon snail

shell 12 cm
high

MOON SNAIL

Polinices lewisii

moon snail
egg castings

clams are the
main prey
of moon
snails by
being
drilled

It is hard to see the stars in action because at low tide, they doze in damp puddles of seaweed and mud under the hot sun or full moon, waiting for the sweet tidal waters to engulf them once again. However, if you go to one of those undersea garden places, you (with 37 other kids) can get a close-up, within one inch of your nose, of a sunflower star charging across the mud bottom when the dinner bell is rung to devour a pound of snail. A sort of Slime Slurp versus the Blob. Twenty-five legs travelling at a foot per second anticipating a juicy lunch is worth the admission fee.

Part of the attraction of the spectacle might be a morbid sense of entertainment in seeing molluscs devoured in such an effective manner — a sort of gladiatorial glee. For my part, I like the sense of ecological paradox — there are no good guys and bad guys in the drama. From a clam's point of view, sunflower stars are both their enemy and their saviour, depending on whether the stars are after them or the Moon Snails. From the snail's point of view, the clams are both their prey and their enemy, since those millions of larvae that the snails secrete are a major source of food for the filter-feeding clams. From the sunflower star's point of view, snails are both prey and enemy, depending on whether the stars are one inch wide or one metre.

So that is why I can look with fondness at my bathroom plunger. In the long, damp winter months I can put it into a prominent position in the bathroom and daydream about the hot, steamy summer dramas where nothing is black and white but clear as mud.

August

HUCKLEBERRY AUGUST:
CHAOS AND HARMONY IN THE CLASSIC PATCH

I seem to spend these long summer evenings at a berry patch along the edge of our road. I stand in it for at least half an hour a day. I notice the odd motorist passing by, narrowing their eyes then accelerating quickly past. I wave and beckon them with my red-stained hands and they accelerate even faster. It is a pity because they might enjoy the odd foray into the patch.

I go there because my ears are filled with the hum of crickets and the chatter of birds, my eyes move hazily from one red or purple jewel to the next and my stomach has the rare delight of being filled with the fruit of our forest, instead of the fruit of yet another banana republic. Our patch is still what would be termed a classic coastal Douglas-fir forest berry patch. This is not the rampant patch one finds overtaking vacant city lots, composed of those interlopers, the Himalayan and the Evergreen Blackberry. These two species are definite challengers in taste and quantity — but for diversity, subtlety and seasonal duration, nothing can beat our classic native berry species.

A classic patch is one which begins with the first blossoming of the Salmonberries in March and extends into the middle of November with the last of the huckleberries and Bunchberries.

Over the last five months, I have been able to complement most evening meals with a modest dessert of sweet and succulent berries of varying size, hue and flavour. Day after day, month after month, I march down to the patch, open my mouth and drop a few in.

I know it is April when the big pink flowers of the Salmonberry wave in my face and the Swainson's Thrush calls to ripen the first berries to orange and red. I know it is May when the delicate white Thimbleberry flowers are dropping off and the blood-red berries are starting to come out. In June, I can glean the last of the Salmonberries, the best of the Thimbleberries and the first of the Blackcap, our native raspberry. By July, I am scouring the ground cover for Trailing Blackberries (our native blackberry, which far exceeds in flavour the exotic species) and Wild Strawberries. For

bulk I'll fill up on Salal berries and for pure sweet, I'll go for the gooseberries. There are two gooseberries, the Wild and the Gummy Gooseberry. Both produce large red berries. The Gummy berries are hairy. By August the Red Huckleberries are out as well and I go searching the northerly, damper patches for the late bloomers. The rest of the autumn I can rely on consistent crops of the Red and Evergreen Huckleberries and Bunchberries until the first frost. Thereupon I cease my visits to the patch and go hibernate like all good berry-eaters.

I like my berry patch because it is a reassuring place to be. Anxieties about war and famine are forgotten in this patch. Sedatives by the thousands are out there for modern anxieties but I prefer the berry patch. It all stems from an influential time in my life when I encountered the Berry People. They hung out in a barn in the 1960s and attempted to live entirely off berries. They ate them, drank their juice, tie-dyed their clothes purple and fuelled a car off berry methane gas. They lasted quite a while before the glamour of a subsistence lifestyle wore off and they retired to their condos in Vancouver with terminal stomach aches and permanently dyed fingers. Back then it was the closest thing to a subsistence culture I had experienced. Later, I was to work with some First Nations Chilcotin people which put the Berry People in their rightful roles as rank amateurs.

Of course the Berry People are gone now and so are most vestiges of true aboriginal way-of-life in this region, but we still have some berry patches left. Not many, but enough to complement a few diets. For an uncertain future this is a reassuring thought. I only have to think of friends in what was once Yugoslavia, supplementing their diet with local berries as the food ran out. Who would have thought that my sophisticated Croatian friends studying law, then wind-surfing in their holidays, would have to reach to their aboriginal roots to survive. So I think of them in my berry patch.

Another reassurance that this patch provides is something to do with the whole biodiversity argument. They say that many of the commercial raspberries, strawberries and gooseberries were hybridized from our native species. In my little thicket of tangled berries, one species entwined with another, tumbling over rotting logs, insects and birds humming around, I know the combination is right for enduring the hazards of nature. It is unlikely that there will be a large-scale insect devastation or blight in this patch because it is chaos. Equilibrium is reached by virtue of thousands of years of confusion. When the commercial hybrids have foundered from over-specialization, the scientists will come back to this thicket.

My final comfort comes from a Chilcotin legend about the repercussions of over-fulfilling one's desires — a tale to be told in the patch. Raven once stole the only Salmonberries on earth from a sacred patch guarded by the people. He laughed so loud, thinking himself clever to steal them, that the berries all fell from his mouth and scattered over the land, springing up as new bushes wherever they fell. Standing amongst the Salmonberries, I felt it was fitting that as a tribute to our cleverness at manipulating the world, we might be left with the odd patch of berries. As those motorists zoom disdainfully by me, I'll have the last laugh.

THE ROLLING TIDES:
GUT-CHURNING ADVENTURES WITH ALGAE

Dinoflagellate. It means fearful, whirling, hairy thing. It is a word you should get used to because you are going to see it more frequently. Don't get your hopes up for Mick Jagger, though; the creature in question is *Alexandrium catanella* — an organism which does have a great deal in common with the Rolling Stones' leading man. Besides being hairy, both have been around for a long time, do the odd tour of the west coast, have toxic properties and send people into delirium after exposure. Where they differ is that M. Jagger's tours are slowing down and *A. catanella*'s are speeding up.

A. catanella and friends are more commonly known as "red tide." They are microscopic algae that "bloom" under certain conditions, producing the red, murky tint to the sea. These small organisms typically float about in reasonable numbers behaving like the mild-mannered plants that they are, but if the water gets above a certain temperature and nutrients become available from converging currents, the population explodes and you end up

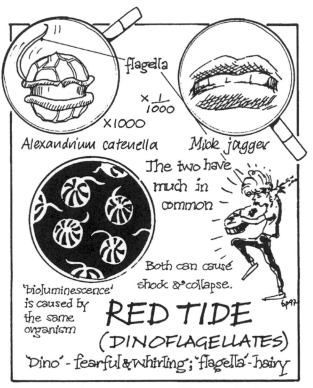

flagella

$\times \frac{1}{1000}$

×1000

Alexandrium catenella

Mick jagger

The two have much in common -

'bioluminescence' is caused by the same organism

Both can cause shock & collapse.

RED TIDE
(DINOFLAGELLATES)

'Dino' - fearful & whirling; 'flagella' - hairy

with millions per litre of water. These algal blooms have probably been occurring since life began; algae are the start of the food chain and turn the wheels of life. What's new is that the toxin-producing species of algae (dinoflagellates and diatoms) are blooming more frequently, more severely and for longer periods of time. The toxins then accumulate in shellfish and, when ingested by organisms like you or me, cause illnesses such as Paralytic Shellfish Poisoning (PSP) and other nasties.

I was swimming in the sea one July day when the red tide arrived. One minute the sea was blue, cool and clear; the next it was red, warm and murky. I churned through the sea and came out covered in a film of slimy dinoflagellates with a diatom hairdo that would have done a Stones' fan proud. In all my life, I don't remember a red tide like this one. Childhood rhymes of "stay wide of red tide" and "don't eat oysters if there isn't an 'r' in the month," i.e., May, June, July, August, filled me with terror.

103

Then there were the scare stories, such as the fishermen who were found dead in their boat off Barkley Sound after having clams for lunch, or Captain Vancouver's first mate who died from eating oysters at Poison Cove. But you actually didn't meet many people who had seen red tide; now it is everywhere. I was on the west coast of the island in October and *A. catanella* was there doing a gig alongside sunfish, tuna and pelicans, all riding the warm currents of El Niño.

Red tide is now becoming such a worry around the world that there are whole websites devoted to the subject. American paranoias have switched from the red tide of communism to the red tide of diatoms ("they can't get no satisfaction"). The causes of the increase in the algal blooms are obvious to anyone who spends lots of time churning away in the tide. The climate is changing, the ocean's currents are doing funny things and we are polluting our earth. In Florida, they have diatoms that are making manatees sick and scaring tourists — rock and roll was never this bad. In the Philippines, Maine and Japan pernicious dinoflagellates are ruining aquaculture — something even communism couldn't do.

In the grand scheme of things, red tide is yet another clue that "you can't always get what you want." Think to yourself: It is time to "get off my cloud" before "it's all over now." Throw less rubbish down your sink; speak out for environmental causes; stop buying plastics and don't go to big-box stores. Take yourself down to the sea and observe what is going on. You can even "spend the night together" as *A. catanella* is the same organism that provides bioluminescence in the ocean at night — those incredible flashes of light whenever a fish or a paddle turns the water. And while you are sitting there with "jumping jack flash," hope that "[tide] is on our side."

PASSIONATE SIGHTSEERS:
GUILLEMOTS AND TERMINAL WILDERNESSES

The air shimmered off the tarmac and pods of visitors lurked in the shade of buses labelled City and Nature Tours, fanning themselves with sightseeing pamphlets from the world-

famous Butchart Gardens in Victoria — their trademark a fluorescent rose. Finally, one brave visitor broke from the group and
followed a hint of breeze, finning her way between parked cars.
Near the shore, she reached a chain-link fence and threw herself
against it like a plastic bag on a windy day. Much revived, she
spotted something in the water and excitedly called to her group.

Within minutes, the entire group had moved to the fence at
the Swartz Bay ferry terminal. I named it the "Fence of a
Thousand Missed Opportunities," the kind often found in ferry
terminals keeping people away from the only natural respite, the
sea. Passengers, while they wait interminably (pun intended), are
generally not encouraged to take their air at the shore but swelter
away on the tarmac or consume insipid coffee inside concrete
boxes marooned in the tarmac. To find the sea, turn your back on
the hot afternoon sun, sniff the air for a tangle of the islands and
walk in that direction. Navigate around the cement waiting
boxes. Keep going until you find the graceful limbs of an
Arbutus/Madrone tree impudently breaking through the chain-
link and you will find the place our excited group gathered.

nest on ledges &
burrows

red feet

PIGEON GUILLEMOT
Cepphus columba
Fall moult

A ferry terminal is never without activity in the waters. It was the lure of one of the inhabitants, a seal pup, that brought this group down. Seal pups are good at luring; they attract mother seals, movie stars and tourists with the bat of an eyelid. And with eyes larger than those of a Jersey cow, there is lots of eyelid — in fact three of them, top, bottom and an eyelid that acts like a windshield wiper. Their eyes are designed to see in air and under water, where they have to hunt without much light, so they dilate their pupils to the huge dark orbs that stop people buying fur coats. This is Harbour Seal pupping time and safe haul-outs away from the intrusions of inquisitive boaters, kayakers and Orcas are hard to find. The ferry docks are probably ideal; the ferries are a known quantity, well-meaning people wanting to rescue them are prevented from so doing by the chain-link fence and Orcas wouldn't stray in amongst the pilings.

Suddenly another member of the group spotted a cluster of sea stars tussling it out on the barnacled rocks. Supercharged with the riotous colours of Butchart's flower beds, the visitors couldn't help but appreciate the joys of mixing inappropriate colours like the Ochre, Vermillion, Pink and Sunflower sea stars. On cue, a Belted Kingfisher chattered across the waters in front of them, landing in the limbs of the Arbutus/Madrone. She then took off again, hovered and speared into the water after a Shiner Perch (more Butchart's inspiration of fluorescent yellow and black). There was a round of applause.

In the background swam a dozen or so Pigeon Guillemots which nest in the metal slots between the pilings — a modern alternative to cliff nesting sites. These sleek little black birds, related to puffins, have white wingbars and are almost always around the docks, ducking under the ferries as if they are casual driftwood floating by. From the Fence of a Thousand Missed Opportunities you can just see the nest slots. If the birds are on their nests you can see their bright red feet that are shoved out in front as a sort of red flag to any predator — few and far between at the ferry. The group spotted the red feet from their vantage point and burst once more into a peal of excited chatter at their good fortune to see red, white and black again in a new juxtaposition other than in a hanging basket.

The hour or so waiting for the ferry passed by quickly with the drama and the splendour of dock life. I talked to a lady from Tasmania, a family from Japan, a couple from Britain and an elderly man from Tennessee who was dressed in honour of every colour he had witnessed that day. They were well pleased with the latter half of their City and Nature Tour and they didn't have to pay a cent for it. We glanced back to the hot temples of coffee wavering above the endless tarmac and felt sorry for the tourists stuck inside. Above us all, the busy ferry executives planned new cement monuments to the aesthetic traditions of island life.

GOOD LUCK SWALLOWS

I breathed a sigh of relief today. The baby swallows fledged and good luck can once again perch upon our house eaves for another year. An element of superstition lurks in most hearts; mine happens to be the ancient belief that if a swallow returns each year to build a nest upon a house then you will be protected from all manner of evils: fire, lightning, developers and editorial rejections. If they fail to return, the omen is bad.

This year was touch and go, a brief brush with fate. In April, we eagerly anticipated the arrival of the swallows. Salish Sea dwellers are lucky enough to get four types of swallows that nest on houses: Violet-green, Tree, Cliff and Barn Swallows. The first sign that the yearly ritual has begun is a brilliant flash of green from the Violet-green Swallows as they check out the nest boxes we built. Next come the even more irridescent Tree Swallows which usually nest in the wildlife tree right next to the house. Finally the Barn Swallows arrive in a chatter, ready to roost in their old place above the window frames. We are a cozy little community living in sweet symbiosis. They have cool, ready-made homes and we are protected from lightning strikes, mad editors and mosquitoes. It seems a fair deal.

At first, all was progressing smoothly this spring. There were the usual courtship tumbles in the sky, the jostling for territory and the lengthy nest site inspections with practice approaches. We humans made our usual profound predictions about the weather by charting the positions of the swallows: the higher the swallow, the higher the pressure and the better the weather. Due to my inability to determine the height of a swallow in a downpour, these predictions were rarely tested, but the ritual was being happily carried out, uninterrupted, until an alarming event occurred.

It was sometime around the early hours of the morning toward the end of April when I heard the simultaneous honking of a Canada Goose, the piercing cry of a Bald Eagle and the cackle of a Common Raven outside my window. I stuck my head out and peered up into the nest boxes that the swallows had been checking out. A *starling* — not a swallow — stared back down at me with a penetrating eye, letting loose its vocabulary of a thousand bird calls.

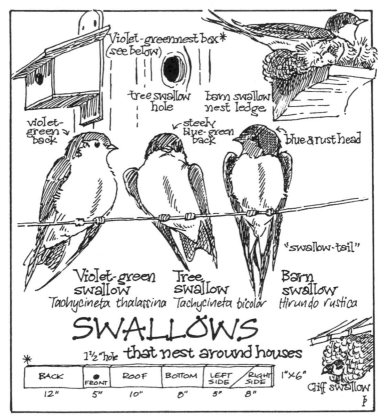

To digress for a moment, one of my greatest fears is a world of starlings and nothing else. European Starlings (*Sturnus vulgaris*) are small, spotted, feisty birds that in a wild Europe before the advent of cities were just one of a diverse group of birds. With the growth of agriculture and cities, starlings adapted well while other species didn't. European cities became dominated by huge roosting flocks of starlings. Even by Shakespeare's time, the starling had taken over London. The starling was described by the character Hotspur, in the play *Henry IV*, as the ultimate weapon to drive the king mad in his sleep. Starlings were imported to North America by a New York romantic in the 19th century who wanted to ensure that all the birds that Shakespeare referred to were present in the New World. This was another well-intentioned action by a deluded, homesick colonist anxious to either improve the literary experiences of the "wild Indians" or drive them mad.

Starlings are survivors *extraordinaire*, following one step behind humans. Every time we open up the forest for our houses and roads, entire tragedies full of Shakespeare's introduced creatures follow us in: "like a rat without a tail," "whoreson caterpillars," "worms, inheritors of the excess," "fall of a [house] sparrow," "pigeon-livered," "daisies pied" and so on. Starlings thrive in suburban and urban areas to the exclusion of just about everything else but pigeons. They will compete very effectively for a variety of nesting sites. I have even seen one starling fight off a pair of flickers twice its size for a nest in a tree hole. Swallows themselves have adapted to urbanization but in a battle between starlings and swallows, the swallows inevitably come out second. Starlings represent the dreariness of a world without diversity.

For me, the arrival of a starling in my eaves was an omen akin to the turning up of the Death Card in a tarot reading. I drank my morning tea with cold dread and prepared some extra fire insurance premiums. I was now condemned to live out eternity in my vision of hell, a devastated landscape populated only by Scotch Broom, thistles and flocks of starlings. The starlings arriving in this previously unstarlinged area were the harbingers of doom, and to make matters worse, I had no one to blame but myself and the very act of being.

This all sets one to wondering about one's rightful place on this earth. After all, we share some remarkably similar characteristics with starlings. We like the same habitat, we compete very effectively with other species, we breed indiscriminately, we spread around the globe and we appear in Shakespeare.

As I morosely pondered whether "to be or not to be" in the dregs of my last cup of tea, I was seized by an overwhelming desire to resist the trend of starlingization. I grabbed my saw and a hand drill and set about furiously refashioning some nest boxes. The one deterrent to starlings is holes that are too small for them, so I devoted the next few hours to adjusting the holes to less than one and a half inches in a star shape — the latest anti-starling fashion. This sort of frenzied behaviour before breakfast is worthy of a Shakespearean comic heroine and more productive than the tragic one flinging herself into a river. The results were almost instantaneous. The interlopers were upstaged and the Violet-green and Tree Swallows were checking out the boxes by that afternoon. The Barn Swallows felt happy amongst their kin and peace was restored.

And so the swallows fledged today. I have had a full two months to watch them hatch and fledge, and ponder my role as divine interventionist in the great comedy of life (must be the Shakespearean influence). As Joseph Meeker said in *The Comedy of Survival*, "the proud visions affirmed by literary tragedy have not led to tragic transcendence, but to ecological catastrophe." With one ecological catastrophe at least deferred for another year, I will watch the swallows head off soon for the tropics and wait patiently for their return next spring before I consider renewing my fire insurance.

SERPENT'S KISS:
PLUMPNESS OF SUMMER, SLIDING INTO WINTER

How would you feel as you slid through the jaws of a snake? This question has cropped up in my life at various times. Usually around August, when the three species of garter snakes along the coast (Common, Northwestern and Western Terrestrial Garter Snakes) have weathered the birth of their young and are all dispersing to sunny promontories near slug-rich forests, sculpin-rich tidepools and/or frog-rich swamps. This is the time when you can observe directly whether a frog, slug, fish or insect confronts its fate with acceptance or denial. When I ask other people the question, it always elicits a powerful response either way. The answer reflects their superstitions toward snakes, which are surprisingly ambivalent.

Good field observations are probably the best foundation upon which to base a superstition: preferably field observations made at an early age so as to prevent any phobias from emerging. Then you are free from prejudice to observe these three beautiful species around the Salish Sea. In real life, I have only ever seen a calm demeanour in a victim as it slides through the jaws. I once surprised a garter snake that had started to eat a slug when it spotted me. The snake decided to retreat and tried to disengorge the slug, which proved harder than it sounds. After

Northwestern Garter Snake.
Indistinct stripes on back & sides in yellow, cream, orange & red...

Red Spotted Garter Snake.
Distinct white back stripe - red spots on sides

up to one metre long

Wandering Garter Snake
Distinct back & side stripes, dark blotchy background colour

Garter Snakes are harmless unless you are a frog, slug, bullhead, etc.

GARTER SNAKES
Thamnophis spp.
From "The Little Prince"

bpenn 97

111

several minutes the snake succeeded, leaving the slug exactly where it had been facing its doom moments before. The slug kept moving, as if there was little difference between sliding through a tunnel of skin or a tunnel of grass. Frogs and fish appear to do the same thing. I haven't witnessed any furious croaking or flapping as they enter the jaws. There is a beautiful sculpture that I once saw of a calm frog in the mouth of a snake. The artist had obviously made similar observations.

It was just as well that I had seen a calm animal in the jaws of a snake by the time I was exposed to *The Little Prince*, by the French writer, Antoine Saint-Exupéry. He kicks off the story with a drawing of a boa constrictor in the act of swallowing an animal. He shows the snake's prey, a mouse, with a frightened look on its face. I don't think Saint Exupéry spent time watching snakes. He could have put me off them for life. I think he was influenced by the strong, snake-fearing traditions that have emerged. In ancient Sumeria, darkness and chaos were represented by the snake. For the Egyptians, Apop, the serpent, was the symbol of all evil. The Hebrews and the Vikings thought the same and Eve certainly was naughty to accept favours from the snake.

On the side of the more empirically based superstitions, the Philistines were deifying snakes for their curative powers. The Greeks, Romans and Celts thought they were the symbol of all fertility. The Egyptians countered their evil snake stories with a serpent that accompanied the sun god Ra and embodied royal power and wisdom. Christians are so ambivalent about snakes that one could grow up feeling very confused about one's faith. Apparently, Christians called Jesus Christ "the Good Serpent." History doesn't relate whether it was he that offered Eve the apple. The Salish are similarly enigmatic in their snake stories. On the one hand, if you rubbed a discarded garter snake skin on your skin it would make you irresistible. On the other hand, there were war-songs warning everyone of the fearless snake people and their double-headed snake gods. One would not be inclined to rub oneself with a snake skin on the day a raiding party chose to strike.

Back to empirical research, it appears that the reason prey rarely express a sense of fear or danger at their captor's jaws is that the snake's capture methods are highly efficient. It's most likely that the calm demeanour of slug, frog or fish persists because they don't know that they are being devoured. Now this is a quality to be greatly upheld in our superstitions. Along with the facts that without reptiles we would be overrun by slugs, rodents and insects; or that they can have 29 babies born live (not as eggs) in one go; or that they spread through the Salish Sea by swimming between islands; or that the flash of their stripes in the bleached blond grasses of summer can fill your mind with beauty. With names such as *Thamnoides elegans,* subspecies *vagrans* (literally the wandering elegant garter snake), they deserve more story myths.

To tell the three species apart is somewhat of a challenge as they are highly variable in colouring, both between species and within local populations. Taxonomists also further serve to confuse us by separating them into more subspecies, which include the Red-spotted Garter Snake. As a rule of thumb, the Common Garter Snakes (*Thamnoides sirtalis*) have seven scales on each side of their upper lip. The Western Terrestrial (*Thamnoides elegans*) have eight. These two species are the ones most likely found in lakes or tidepools. The Northwestern Garter Snake (*Thamnoides ordinoides*) is actually the most common snake in the region; they have eight scales on their lower lip and they aren't as fond of water.

With the days still hot but the nights starting to cool, the elegant scaled ones can be seen heading each morning to the rock piles to warm up. They lie so relaxed, casually coiled and deeply appreciative of the warmth seeping through their scales, that I can warm to the Egyptians and their sun god story. Unfortunately, their desire for warm places leads snakes onto roads — the true hell. This leads me to wish for the day when a superstition causes people to drive at ten kilometres per hour in August so as to avoid basking snakes. If you are an impatient sort of person with chronic road rage, then you would do well to take an interest in the future of these reptiles. It would help you appreciate those who drive slowly. You might even find yourself pulling over to rescue a snake and ponder your simultaneous admiration and fear of the great mysteries of life.

September

LOSING MARMOTS: POLITICOS, GYROS AND THE FUTURE

Over the last eight years I have written several articles on the Vancouver Island Marmot — one of the world's most endangered mammals, native only to Vancouver Island. About every two years, I get a hankering to provide an update on how they are doing. The first time I wrote about them, the population was estimated to be between 200 and 300. That column was written as September frosts of 1994 were just touching the mountaintops between Nanaimo and Strathcona where they live. Half the marmots were heading down traditional burrows in the sub-alpine meadows for their winter hibernation. The other half were heading down burrows constructed in clearcuts. What had been discovered was that the marmots were using clearcuts like alpine meadows and the population was declining because of it.

The 1994 story was pitched as a good-news story because a strategy had been proposed for reintroducing these distinctive, chocolate-brown mammals into some of their traditional meadow colonies to increase the chances of their survival. In 1996, the article was a mildly good-news story in that a reintroduction was finally conducted in the summer. However, I had to report that there weren't very many animals to transplant — numbers had dropped to less than 150 — and the clearcuts still needed 97 years to grow back. In 1998, I wrote another story that was closer to a dirge than anything. Numbers were down to less than 75 and reintroductions were unsuccessful. Animals were now being airlifted by helicopter to zoos for the captive-breeding program. What little joys were awaiting millennium articles, I wondered. Marmot-writing is a form of masochism. Sort of like falling in love with someone on death row.

Vancouver Island Marmots were "officially" discovered within the scientific community by a collector, Harry Swarth, on a mountain near Port Alberni in 1910. Swarth shot 11 marmots with white muzzles in the name of science and revealed to the world that Vancouver Island had a distinct species that had evolved in isolation in our sub-alpine meadows.

< 150... ∨ left... on earth ...

'Bob Dole' on the watch for eagles.

Traditional habitat is subalpine meadows.

VANCOUVER ISLAND MARMOT

Marmota vancouverensis

First Nations had obviously discovered marmots a few years earlier, as archaeologists have found five sites with middens of marmot bones, some dating back to nearly 3,000 years ago. Why these early cultures, with the bounty of the coast at their disposal, would go after a handful of marmots in remote mountainous areas is open for conjecture. Scientists have a theory about medicinal uses. In Siberia, where there are similar species, they have traditional marmot recipes for a host of ailments.

Historically, the marmots survived these little hunting forays. As a survival mechanism, marmots are experts at dispersing and reestablishing colonies in widely separated sub-alpine meadows surrounded by miles of forested mountain valleys. Young breeding adults typically leave a colony in their second or third year and travel miles until they get to another nice sunny slope with lots of wildflowers and secure dens to sleep in. In the natural course of things, colonies probably came and went. Even one family of Golden Eagles could do damage to a marmot colony but there was always some young blood to move in and fill the niche.

A classic marmot colony can be found along a mountain ridge above 1,000 metres, somewhere like Strathcona Park. Marmot meadows are characterized by a good mix of wildflowers and boulders under which marmots can escape from marauding eagles. Imagine loud whistles of the marmots ringing across the crisp mountain air as you amble amongst the Tiger Lilies, Pearly Everlasting and huckleberries. Stretch yourself out on a boulder and look down at the view below of lichen-covered Mountain Hemlocks rising up through the valley mists. Listen for the Roosevelt's Elk bugling to each other.

So why aren't the marmots still in places like Strathcona Park? This is the paradox. There haven't been any direct changes to traditional marmot habitat itself in the park. Many of their colonies in meadows have remained unchanged as neither boulders nor wildflowers have been marketable commodities. What has changed is that the forested valleys in between have largely been logged or cleared for ski runs and the marmots have discovered a new type of habitat — clearcuts. Half the world's population of marmots now live in clearcuts. So, one would think that if marmots could adapt successfully to clearcuts, we would have more marmots than starlings — but we don't.

The marmots were declared a rare and endangered species officially in 1980 when the newly formed Vancouver Island Marmot Preservation Committee declared that "it is an animal set up for extinction and it may be beyond our capacity to do anything about it. Man is moving into the mountains in ever increasing numbers." A young scientist, Andrew Bryant, banked his career on his capacity to do something about it. Through a rigorous regime of monitoring individuals with tags and transmitters, he discovered the reasons why there are important differences between the clearcut colonies and the alpine colonies — research which would go on to justify a recovery program.

Over eight years, Andrew documented that marmots never lived past five years of age in a clearcut. They only reach sexual maturity at four. Andrew hypothesized that the traditional meadows were the supply of new marmots and the clearcuts were the sinks. Clearcuts are misleading and unstable places. They look like alpine meadows to a marmot but they aren't, and if you are spending six months of your year in bed with no food, you don't have a lot of tolerance for flash floods or shifting ice packs. On top of that, logging roads are like superhighways for cougars and wolves to these marmot restaurants.

Phase 1 of the recovery strategy involved helicopters transporting some marmots across those clearcuts to traditional marmot colony sites where they could reestablish themselves. In 1996, six were transported to a traditional site. They all died. When a marmot colony disappears on a mountaintop, the mountain dies a bit, too. I only ever spent a day with the marmots but it was enough to imagine the consequences of extinction. The air stops ringing with the whistles, the soil loses the rich droppings, the seeds aren't dispersed, the eagles lose their prey and the small, gentle, courtship dances are lost to memory forever.

The recovery team is still involved in an intensive program of relocations, a pilot captive-breeding program at the Toronto and Calgary zoos and a captive-breeding facility constructed on Vancouver Island. When I spoke to Andrew in 1999 about the expectations of the recovery plan he had three things to say. The population is at such a low point that there is nothing to lose and everything to gain by trying a variety of ways to save them. The Russians and Europeans saved their marmots by a breeding and reintroduction program. Zoos can apparently keep the species from extinction until the forests grow back and we adopt better forest practices on private and public lands. He didn't anticipate a rapid recovery.

When I first wrote about marmots, I noted that, with their fat whiskered cheeks, they looked like one of those fat whiskered politicians of my childhood in the 1960s. The type who promised us a rich metropolis of houses with cellulose drapes and private helicopters. All we needed to do was extract the rich resources from shore to mountain. The politicians largely got their way but the small irony I took comfort in was that a bunch of marmots were more likely to be living in a rich metropolis and flying around in a helicopter than me — which still continues to give me grounds for a good-news story.

WARHOL'S SALMON: FAME FOR FIFTEEN MINUTES

When artist Andy Warhol recreated the image of a Campbell's soup tin, he was hoping for a reaction to the age of mass production. I know I have never looked at a tin of soup in the same way since. The soup even began to taste different. It had the flavour of loss. It tasted like the end of home cooking and gathered foods.

If Andy Warhol had been dropped onto the west coast instead of Manhattan, I wonder what he would have done with a can of salmon — the Campbell's soup tin of the rainforest. He might have recognized the romance of the fish and the need for us to look at it differently the next time we took one out of the cupboard.

After all, Andy immortalized Marilyn Monroe — and she and salmon have a lot in common. Both are beautiful, with lush lips, hooded eyes and big teeth. They both steam with sensuality. When you sit by a creek where the Coho are spawning, the air is heavy with their energy. Female tails drum at the stones to create spawning nests or "redds," in which to lay their eggs, while the curving jaws of the males rake at the water to get enough oxygen to push them to the end. Their massive, muscular bodies move from saltwater sea to freshwater creek and transform in front of your eyes. Lipstick crimsons, eyeshadow blues and nail-polish greens freckle their bodies and leave them as beautiful as a Marilyn in a lush, dappled creek bed.

Warhol would have pondered how to catch that moment of sensuality — trying to find a way to express the inexpressible in an image that has already clogged our minds with repetition. How many salmon have you seen, alive or dead, canned or frozen, baked or fricasseed, in the newspaper or on television, in shop windows or on billboards? How easy is it to think of them as as dull as a Campbell's soup? What would it take to make us see them differently?

I have asked lots of people this question. Andy Warhol would really have been no help: he's dead anyway and probably would have been put off by the rain and lack of groupies. There are no swarms of *paparazzi* around salmon. There are swarms of everything else though: River Otters, Raccoons, Black and Grizzly Bears, Pine Martens, gulls, eagles, shrews, mice, Steller's Jays, Shore Crabs, flies, carrion beetles, ravens and crows. And then there is the swarm of waterlogged green desperados and itinerant artists who are under the spell of wild, unlogged estuaries along the coast — wondering what it is going to take to tell this story so that there is a reaction from people, with the flavour of loss if we don't do something.

Among the desperado filmmakers, photographers, writers and artists I have met wandering around the coast, not one of them has felt they ever did the spectacle of a salmon spawn justice. For me, an itinerant journalist with pen and ink, the rainforest is evasive. Rain is incessant, you can only bring out your sketch book one day in ten and even then, the damp seeps into the linen rag of the paper and swells it like the Western Redcedars so that any pencil mark becomes a groove. A groove to depict a bear, a Devil's Club groove, a Banana Slug groove. Then you start to wonder why you are leaving grooves on paper and not on cedar. Traditional carving begins to make sense and Warhol silkscreens fade totally out of the picture. Not being a carver, I started looking around for other media.

One day in Roscoe Inlet, Heiltsuk territory, or the Great Bear Rain Forest, I discovered my medium. Everywhere, there were pots of paint in the flesh of dead and decaying Chum and Coho Salmon hauled onto the land by tides, Grizzly Bears, Wolves and Bald Eagles. Blank flat canvases of salt-grass marshes or moss floors presented endless opportunities. We created a tableau across the bleached salt grass, the passage of a salmon from the last death throes to the skeleton — a process that takes about nine days and is one of the wonders of the world.

When you paint with fish on an estuary canvas, you have to be prepared for a day of the senses. First, you have to get used to the smell. The smell is so rank and unforgettable that your nose overcomes your eyes and you have to remind yourself which part of the face is in charge. Not surprisingly, there were few groupies for this art installation. Ian McAllister, co-author and photographer of *The Great Bear Rainforest* and desperado, was roped in. We selected nine salmon in nine different stages of decay and

CHUM SALMON &
SITKA SPRUCE

'fish grow on trees..
trees grow on fish'

lined them up, nose to tail, to illustrate the progression of nutrients from the water to the land. We started the first at the water's edge and laid the salmon in a line to a spruce tree where the life of the river was taken up through its roots.

For the visually inspired, the first fish had pomegranate gills and flesh where it had rubbed itself raw. Baby-blush pink eggs clung to the female's spent body. Corvette bluebottle flies sparkled in the cavernous mouth. Decay dimmed the reds but flourished in the whites and greens until the last fish — a bleached skeleton with a dried, black, leathery skin curled around it. You could tell it was a male by the huge, hooked fighting teeth jutting up like the paps of Marilyn. The sound was steamy too. Ravens and Steller's Jays were ecstatic, Varied Thrushes were whistling and the thrash of the live salmon beating their way up through the stones added percussion to the mad opera of the river. Manhattan and the throb of a city seemed mild in comparison.

We finished laying the last skeleton of salmon around the base of the Sitka Spruce where crumpled Lady Ferns, amongst the moss, held the mark of a grizzly's early morning breakfast. The painting was complete; it went no further than the estuary. What drove damp desperados to create an installation that few saw and would be rearranged by bears and tide by morning? For us it intimated the romance of the fish, the mysterious ways in which it connected the land and the sea and ourselves — the realization that salmon feed everything from the flies to the spruce. Laying them across the land, from sea to tree, was a way to describe the ecological process that has created the richness of the rainforest. If nothing else, it wasn't replicated a hundred thousand times on paper made from old-growth forests — and, as Warhol predicted, the salmon were famous for 15 minutes.

TALE OF TAILS: THE TAMING OF THE SHREW

There is a rock outside our kitchen door, left by a passing glacier. Geologists call it an erratic; we call it Theatre Rock because there is a performance around it every day. The curtains rise at eight o'clock, when the last crumb of breakfast has been swept out the door to fly ceremoniously around the Rock. The play varies a bit through the seasons, but generally it follows the same themes: love, war, tragedy and comedy. What it has never featured is the taming of the shrew.

Dusky Shrews are one of the main characters in this ongoing drama. The other roles are played by our native scavengers, the Song Sparrows and Deer Mice, and a summer house guest unused to wildlife. There is an intricate relationship between all four of the groups throughout the plot, which is performed in five acts. The first act opens as the dust settles around Theatre Rock, after the crumbs have landed, and the house guest settles

Native species that hang around the house.

HOUSE GUESTS

Song Sparrow
Melospiza melodia

look for the large dark spot on the chest

mice with wings

11-20 cms.

deer mice are omnivorous

Deer Mice
Peromyscus maniculatus

Dusky Shrew
Sorex monticolus

9-11 cm

shrews wear out not rust out

himself atop the Rock for a first communion with nature. Enter stage right a shrew. Enter stage left another shrew. Exit stage right the house guest back through the kitchen door. A battle scene starts. The protagonist and the antagonist are difficult to distinguish until their tiny eyeballs meet over the edge of a crust. An operatic duet starts at this point.

After several minutes of competing sopranos, the battle scene resumes. It is earnest with no attempt at negotiations (it is not a '90s drama). There are three fates a shrew may face — another shrew, another shrew or another shrew. While the battle rages on, the house guest reenters to provide a running commentary, but at a safe distance. Enter from upstage centre a Song Sparrow (flying mouse) who sings the joys of divide and conquer in an aria, while she quickly finishes off what the shrews were fighting over. Tragedy ensues. The hero, now recognizable by his suffering, lies gasping in the dust while the sun moves slowly overhead. The two warriors retreat to the shadow of Theatre Rock.

The second act reveals the tragic flaw of the sparrow. Unsatisfied with the crumbs around Theatre Rock, she looks for the source of more crumbs. Eyeing the open kitchen door, her appetite drives her onward and inward to the house. Once in the house, three fates await her — a glass window, a freshly swept floor or the house guest. The audience is left wondering about her fate and the scene switches back to the Rock.

The vanquished shrew has now recovered and returns timidly to the battleground. A New Age female rushes to her man and they put their differences between them, so to speak. The house guest reenters the stage, casting his large shadow over the love nest. The hero, detecting a challenge to his manhood, runs at the house guest. Exit quickly house guest.

Third act, in the house. A meal has been devoured and the remains are lying around on the table. The sparrow has escaped two of the three fates. She is gleaning the crumbs from the floor when the house guest takes up a broom. It is left up to the audience to decide whether the brush is meant for the sparrow or the crumbs.

Dusk is approaching and the shrews have retreated for the evening, leaving the avenue clear for the Deer Mice. The mice appear to have spent the previous two acts planning their strategy to optimize their share of crumbs. They have figured out that crumbs do not emanate from the floor but from the cupboards too. They are equitable mice and collectively finish off the crumbs from the dinner around Theatre Rock, then exit centre stage — in through the open door.

Fourth act. The house guest has disappeared temporarily, only to be seen standing on top of Theatre Rock. The sparrow is back outside getting ready to roost alongside the house guest. The mice are busy running through cupboards, floors and doors. They have three fates — the live trap, a clean house or a vindictive house guest. The first is a good possibility, the second an impossibility. The tension builds to see what the *dénouement* will be.

Fifth act. The human house guest, who is now an outside guest, begins to sing a solo from the Rock. He sings about his three fates — shrews, mice or sparrows. He exits with his tail between his legs, never to be seen again, and returns to the safe, clean city. The mice, although clever, are not clever enough and succumb to their first fate after only half an evening's foraging is complete. The sparrow continues to hop between the kitchen floor and Theatre Rock, driven by the dream of a better meal. And the shrews continue to emerge from Theatre Rock, when the dust settles, to fight, eat and mate. The morals of the play: some house guests are more tolerant than others, you can never get all the crumbs and you will never tame the shrew.

RAISING THE DEAD:
BETTER BURIALS THROUGH TURKEY VULTURES

There is no doubt in my mind about which type of vulture I want attendant upon my death. Any funeral industry catalogue will provide you with a long list of the unwelcome vultures. A book on the birds of the west coast will supply you with the one species I would be happy to have pick over my bones — the Turkey Vulture. There are few selfless acts toward the natural world available to human beings and the one that would cause us the least inconvenience is illegal — the simple act of being consumed by nature's prime scavengers.

This is an ancient tradition. Very clean, very quick and very apt. One minute you are upon the ground, the next you are skyward, soaring with absolute silence above the mad machinations of our frenzied little earth. There is no blazing inferno to anticipate or dank, black cold with secular worms. Flesh moves quickly from one earth form to an aerial other. Parsees call it a sky burial. Buddhists call it the reunion with the cosmos. Egyptians and Mayans saw it as the passage of the corporeal

teeters like a kite

wings are 2-toned
tiny head

soars with wings in a shallow 'V'

TURKEY VULTURE

Cathartes aura
symbol of rebirth

Most arrive in April to breed, leave in Oct. for the south.

redhead

bodies into the realm of the gods. Aboriginal cultures around the world venerated the vulture and we, the secular west, close our eyes and shudder.

Turkey Vultures are definitely my first choice for a reincarnation. For a start, they nest a moment's flight from my house on an ancient piece of Wrangellian lava rising up out of the Salish Sea that no one can reach except the most intransigent Garry Oaks and stalwart Northern Alligator Lizards. What companions for my next flight through time! They mate for life so there is no chance of an emotional wrench to mar our courting on the thermals above the cliffs. I would lay one or two eggs every second year on a rocky ledge that required no housekeeping. The brooding responsibilities of the chick(s) are equally shared with my mate.

During the day we would soar over the forests and meadows of the islands of the Salish Sea scanning the landscape with our noses and eyes for the effervescent whiff of a rotting fawn or a sheep's afterbirth. We would follow the haying tractors for the occasional garter snake and vole thrown up in the blades. Our friends and relations would politely bow to the first-come, first-served principle but gladly share their food sources with us. Along the coast a rotting fish might tease our tastebuds, then gorged, we would return to the little, white, fluffy nestling(s) and regurgitate the extra into its/their gaping mouth(s).

At night, we would all roost together, watching the sun sink behind the mountains and enjoying the radiant heat of the rocks long after the night has enclosed us. And so the summer would continue until the Bigleaf Maples turn gold. Banding together in ever-increasing circles, we would spiral southward over East Sooke to the Olympics and then down the coast to follow the sun to the Baja.

Not a bad life really, if I could just arrange it. There are a couple of obstacles. For a start, vultures on the whole are not doing well, which is surprising given our wasteful society. New-world vultures have been declining since the halcyon days of the Woolly Mammoth and Bison. The California Condor, a big cousin of the Turkey Vulture, is on the brink of extinction and is hanging on only through a program of zoo rearing and reintroduction. Likewise the Andean Condor, an even bigger cousin in South America. A small cousin, the Black Vulture, is a coastal bird and prowls the Atlantic shoreline for coastal carcasses. It is not doing too badly but, like east coast fishermen, it is having to go the extra distance to find its food.

The Turkey Vulture's hold is precariously linked to sheep farming, deer populations and lack of disturbance in key breeding areas around the rocky bluffs of the Salish Sea. With farmers having to turn into developers every day of the week, it is unlikely that we'll have any sheep carcasses and isolated places into the next millennium. All these birds are hopelessly defence-less in the face of global climate change, poisons, shotguns and shopping malls.

In Europe the vultures are all but extinct. Where once Bearded Vultures gathered to clean up the dead sheep, deer and soldiers left in the fields, there is nothing but starlings swarming over the fields of herbicide-ridden canola. The Bearded Vulture and the Egyptian Vulture are down to fewer than 100 pairs. That leaves only a handful of places to die where there are still viable popu-lations of vultures. The Rift Valley in East Africa, the birthplace of humans, is one attractive option. In fact, it was while standing at the side of a Wildebeest as a covey of vultures ripped into its carcass and stripped it clean within hours under the shade of an acacia tree that I decided that was how I wanted to end my days. The best bet, though, is probably Tibet or Bombay where human bodies sustain those vulture populations.

The unlikelihood of travelling to remote places as I gasp my last puts me in mind of tackling the real obstacle — western aversions to our natural place on this earth. Why is it not against the law for the funeral industry to strip dignity from a body and relegate it to a small metal box that will never contribute to the wing of a great soaring vulture? And why is it not against the law to destroy an endangered species or its habitat? And why is it against the law to return just a morsel of the riches that we have taken from this earth and leave our bodies to the vultures when we die?

October

SUMMER'S END:
TERMITES AND HUMANS SHED THEIR WINGS

For most of us, it is a struggle to discard our wings — the wings that take us up into the ozone for our first bites at wild, licentious living. I discarded my wings grudgingly as the weight of diapers, telephone bills and a conscience for global responsibility dragged me, heels first, back to the ground. I'm sure it was not a pretty sight, with much wailing and gnashing of teeth. If only I could have done it as it really should be done — like the termites, during their rite of passage.

I didn't notice them at first, as I was too busy with my nose in the clouds and heels on the ground, mourning the loss of summer, youth, ozone and everything else in the great pathos of life. It has something to do with October — a time when we take up amateur philosophy. I was boring my young companion with this when he interrupted with a small observation about the "flying ants." I managed to adjust my point of view back to earth and take in the drama that was enacting itself around me. As the ground came into focus, I noticed I was walking on a carpet of wings — gossamer wings with golden threads. And beyond, stepping briskly away from the tangle of wings with never a glance back, were the termites.

What these termites were doing was completing an important stage in the amazing life cycle of a colony (a history that makes our colonization boring by comparison since termites form complex societies and sustain forests). The swarming of a colony is also the only time we really get to see these wonderful insects, unless you are in the habit of poking around rotting houses or stumps.

For those nervous house owners, Pacific Dampwood Termites (*Zootermopsis angusticollis*) are essentially a forest species. If they come upon damp wood in contact with the soil, then they will not distinguish between whether the wood is part of your house or a log. But generally, if your wooden house is dry and not rotting into the ground, you will not have a problem with Dampwood Termites. There is another kind of termite that is much less common on the coast that can burrow through cracks in foundations to reach damp wood but these subterranean termites don't pose a threat to most households. If you have a leaking faucet in a bathroom causing rot, there is a chance that a stray couple of termites might take up residence. Termites are a good sign that

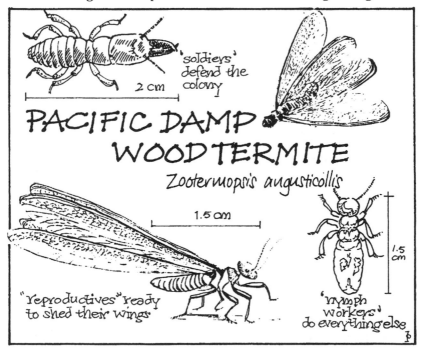

soldiers' defend the colony
2 cm

PACIFIC DAMP WOOD TERMITE

Zootermopsis angusticollis

1.5 cm

1.5 cm

"reproductives" ready to shed their wings.

'nymph workers' do everything else

you need to do some house maintenance — a helpful reminder. Once you sort out the damp, the termites will move on to other, greener pastures as they cannot live on dry wood.

Back to the life cycle: the swarms that are going on all over this region about now are the dance of the young reproductive generation approaching maturity; they are now ready to spread their wings, go out into the wide world, find their mate and a stump, and start a new colony. And what a flight they have. They all gather at the entrance to the colony waiting for dusk, emitting hormones or pheromones in the twilight. At the right moment they all set off in a big swarm. They flirt, they fly, they soar and glide high above the earth. They check out all the action and get high on the sexy, sweaty smells of each other. They fly over the thousands and thousands of stumps and rotting houses until they spy out the perfect nest. Then, floating down with their chosen one, they drop to the earth and step out of their flying garb. That is the moment that confounds me. It is so beautifully executed. They land and just neatly jettison their wings and move on.

While I was still weeping into the debris of scattered wings and lost youth, King and Queen Pacific Dampwood Termite were already investigating the foundation of my house and surrounding forest debris, looking for a good place to rear their colony. The king is very dutiful and assists the queen to get the whole place up and running. Then he mates with her over a number of occasions to begin the brood that will eventually become this complex society of workers, soldiers and the next generation of breeding youths. The workers and the soldiers are blind individuals with either big heads or big teeth who do all the work and defend the colony. They feed and tidy up for the royal family and the young. Termite social organization is a state to which I could easily aspire provided I was a member of the royal family.

The king and queen team up and burrow into the earth very quickly, so watching a swarm is a short-lived pleasure of the end of summer. There are also lots of other things watching these termites. Flickers, sparrows, frogs, garter snakes — anything that eats insects loves them. For every king and queen that make it safely over their nuptial threshold, thousands end up as dinner for the animal kingdom — I include my children and pest exterminators in the latter category. It is their very vulnerability that makes the termites move so fast and dispells any notions of sentimentality about their rite of passage. I envy a termite that.

So watch out for a swarm around now. Go to a place that has lots of rotting wood and you might be rewarded. Alternatively, put a few rotting planks in your backyard and attract them. They'll produce the finest soil you'll ever have. Marvel at the balletic jettisoning of wings and acquire the grace of putting another summer behind you. In the course of all this noble activity, I discovered that my small companion had collected a jar full of termites and released them in the house where I cannot locate them. I take solace from the fact that this house and its occupants will one day be soil; we'll have passed in a dignified fashion from one state to the next in that final rite of passage.

ACORNS AND OTHER LITTLE NUTS: A MONTH TO REMEMBER

There is something compelling about an acorn. This time of year, when they are usually falling around our feet, I can't even pass one by without picking it up and having a look. It is a minor obsession but I think it lurks in some of our genes. The fruit of oaks, including our own native Garry Oak, has been a pivot around which organisms down the west coast from here to California have revolved for millennia. It has only been in the last century that humans have dropped off that list of fans. We found better things to feed and amuse ourselves with, I guess — pizzas and Nintendo.

As an obsession it is not a bad one. I don't go cross-eyed playing with them or get pimples eating them. Mostly I collect them, grow them or hand them out to unjaded children and old ladies to grow. The Garry Oak meadow is an endangered ecosystem and growing the trees is a first step. It is a pleasant pastime and never dull — acorns attract life. I usually start on my hands and knees underneath trees in people's gardens, plucking them from under the leaves. I always ask permission and people invite me in for cups of tea. Sometimes I hang upside down in the trees on road verges and wing the acorns off the branches into a bag below. Passers-by think I am busking or starving and throw quarters in the bag too.

Up in the trees, I get a better vantage point for watching everything else that revolves around the acorns. Generally, I am competing with Steller's Jays, the migratory Band-tailed Pigeons and Northwestern Crows. Steller's Jays are my stiffest competition. They grab those acorns, then fly off to some little cache to store them. The fact that they sometimes forget where their caches are results in new oak groves so I yield to the professionals. Crows do a class act of casually dropping the acorn to

The characteristic silhouette of our only native oak on the coast—gnarled & craggy. This one is on Transit Road near Beach Drive. Victoria.

Stellers jays are important distributors of acorns

Look for the distinctive wavy leaf and acorns. Look for germinating acorns this time of year and protect them

GARRY OAK
Quercus garryana

shatter on the pavement below and then gorging on the sweet flesh. On expeditions to the wilder meadows, I'll sit in a tree at dusk and keep Deer Mice, Raccoons and Blacktail Deer company as they nibble away at the feast.

Because they are being collected for growing, I am fussier than most about my acorns. I don't want ones with weevils or worms. Every second one has some insect firmly attached to this cornucopia, so I assist the nutrient cycle by flinging the blighted ones into the soil to propagate another cycle of wildflowers. This is perhaps the only moment of true purposefulness I might have in the year. With a bulging bag of acorns collected, it is time to disperse them to a new generation of growers. I have never seen the acorns fail to interest a group of eight year olds. You grip their attention with the notion that "little nuts grow into mighty oaks." This hopeful maxim reassures at least the young idealistic misfits. Then you throw your bag of acorns out to the crowd. Like a flock of jays, kids descend on them.

You can demonstrate the genetic diversity of the acorn by asking the young people to what use they would put the acorn. There is always a group of enterprising boys who place their textbooks on top of a handful of acorns and skateboard around the room. Then there is the group of practical young people who promptly crack open the shells with their friends' heads and pop the nut into their mouths. Of this group there are those who check the kernel for worms and weevils and those who never imagine that life could be blemished in any way.

I once watched a little girl happily toss a nut into her mouth, only to find half a weevil left in the shell. She issued a piercing scream and stared transfixed at the source of her horror until the anxious twists of the worm caused her to rescue it from the perils of the skateboarders. Then there is always the group who receive the acorns like newborn babies and anxiously inquire how to nurture them into oaks.

It takes all kinds — and acorns in their quantity seem to accommodate all needs. Back in my tree the other evening, it began to get dark and I noticed the constellation of Libra rise in the night sky. It is a small constellation of about four stars arranged in a circle and it struck me that it formed a perfect acorn (I told you it was only a minor obsession). I have never been that fond of the Babylonian zodiac of judicial scales, exotic scorpions and men with horse costumes on, so I have adopted the acorn as my sign for this month — a regional revision. It will be an easy one to remember and nothing I can think of is quite so generous in its virtues as this little nut.

ARACHNOPHILIA: PIRATES AND SPIDER TREASURES

He was a superstitious Creole pirate who sailed a 16-foot sloop in the Caribbean Sea. She was a small, Jamaican-bred beauty who lived in hope of adventure and fear of the spider. They met at a tropical quay and went on a voyage to the islands where the manatees play. Accompanying them were their faithful travelling companions. He met her companion at the quay — I could introduce myself. She didn't meet his companion — a Giant Crab Spider — until we were well out to sea. Somewhere before the manatee grounds, she discovered the spider and began to scream like the hurricane winds that blow down the palm-lined shores. I, being her faithful travelling companion, was forced to take remedial action and promptly clubbed the poor thing to death. The Creole pirate thereupon rose with such colossal fury for bringing on the evil eye that the hurricane screams halted in mid-roar. The now less-than-faithful companion promptly threatened to jump ship — 16 feet leaves no room for bad feelings. Emotions were eventually brought under control and we made it back to the quay.

This is a true story that took place off the coast of Belize, two decades back, which I tell to demonstrate the powerful mythology of the spider and the incredible range of human emotions attached to them. There are very few half measures in human attitudes to spiders. There is either intense hate or intense love: there is no indifference. The four victims of this story all succumbed to our respective fates. The spider died. The pirate, who revered the spiders for their ability to ward off the evil eye and eat cockroaches, felt the evil eye. The Jamaican beauty, a victim of arachnophobia — the largely irrational fear of spiders that has been documented worldwide over thousands of years — reinforced her phobia. I, a firm believer in seven years bad luck for killing a spider, had seven ill-fated bad years.

Having paid my penance for that rash swatting of the spider and having vowed never to harm one again, I am sensitized to the plight of the spider and never more so than at this time of year when the heavy dews of autumn hang the webs of our spiders with jewel-like beads of water. Most of these webs belong to one of the orb weavers — the ubiquitous Garden Spider (*Araneus diadematus*) which is found throughout the northern hemisphere. They are the ones that have the little white cross on their backs; they have gone into space with the astronauts and scared Miss Muffet (the daughter of Dr. Mouffet, the renowned 16th-century spiderologist). The question is, why should Miss Muffet have been scared away, when spiders do far more to protect our health than threaten it?

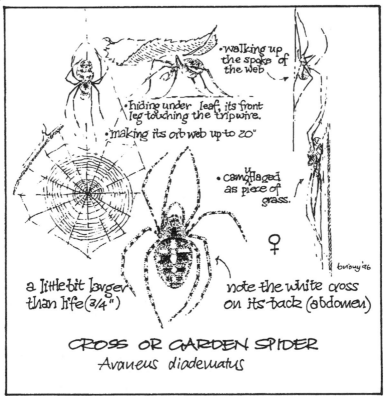

walking up the spoke of the web

• hiding under leaf, its front leg touching the tripwire.

• making its orb web up to 20"

• camouflaged as piece of grass.

♀

bri'ouy '96

a little bit larger than life (3/4")

note the white cross on its back (abdomen)

CROSS OR GARDEN SPIDER
Araneus diadematus

On the coast, we have thousands of types of spiders (identified and unidentified) and the only one that is venomous is the Black Widow Spider, a member of the *Latrodectus* genus. They are very timid and although the bite can be fatal in certain instances, the odds of getting bitten are far lower than being abducted by a Creole pirate. Only the females bite and they are less than half an inch long. They are also easily identifiable, with a red hourglass mark on their underside. Most of the spiders on the coast are harmless, fascinating creatures without whom we would probably be smothered under a mountain of flies.

Spiders are one of the most successful groups of animals on earth, having survived for over 300,000,000 years and having colonized most kinds of habitat on the earth, from glaciers to volcanoes. To give you an indication of their success, the very first form of life to settle Krakatoa, the volcanic island that erupted in 1884, was a tiny spider that ballooned there under its own silk. He beat the naturalist there.

Now is the time to discover why these animals are so successful. The females are getting fattened up for courtship, mating with the males and then producing their egg sacs before dying. Morning is the best time to navigate confidently around them in the grass and avoid more ill omens. Spend a few hours watching them this autumn and figure out the answers to puzzling spider questions. For example, do spiders really eat their mates? How do spiders fly to islands? Why don't they get caught in their own webs? And why, in the grand scheme of things, are pirates, hurricanes, spider killers and superstitions far greater risks to life and limb than the common or Garden Spider?

Maple Leaf Rag: Leaf Me Alone

Sex and politics were the only conversation topics I used to avoid at polite parties. But now I am adding leaves to that list. Leaves are not inherently controversial; it is just that they evoke complicated emotions. First, there's the tension between those who like the leaf on the flag and those who don't — and that is getting more complicated, especially in Quebec. And then there is the division between those who want to get rid of leaves and those who leave them on the ground for posterity — and that is getting more divisive every day.

I have always taken the word "leaves" in its literal sense, as in "leave them where they are." I'm a dead give-away as a leaf leaver; I have leaves pinned to my chest and gumboots stuck to my feet and I hiss whenever I see a leafblower. As far as the maple leaf on the Canadian flag goes, I feel quite proud that as a nation we aspire to a humble leaf instead of a distant galaxy of stars or some rampant lion. But I didn't know I felt so strongly about the subject until I was caught by a surprise question at a party. "Don't you find these enormous leaves are a real nuisance to rake up and get rid of?" a woman innocently asked, pointing to the baroque canopy of gold, red and orange maple leaves draped around us.

She was from California, and they are a bit funny down there. They invented pink stucco and talk about nothing but sex at parties. But something snapped when she raised the question and I ended up in a tirade against everything from free trade to the extinction of amphibians. There were probably a few invectives thrown at leafblowers too. It was quite a performance. She quickly moved on to the next guest.

In hindsight, things could have been handled much better. She probably didn't know they were maple leaves pinned to my Canadian heart. She certainly didn't know it was a Bigleaf Maple, the biggest-leafed maple in Canada, that every west coaster boasts about and presses between two sheets of wax paper in kindergarten. She probably wasn't used to real autumns where the days are so moist and tranquil that you slide through them like a Banana Slug over Skunk Cabbage. I could also forgive her for not recognizing the signs of a person who leaves leaves. I had left my gumboots and my religion at the door.

Now I have had time to calm down and prepare what I would like to have said. "Funny big leaves aren't they? Whenever I used to see the pictures of Adam, I wondered what would have happened if he had worn a Bigleaf Maple. Eve would never have been tempted and everyone would be in the Garden of Eden instead of just us lotus eaters on the coast. The biggest one ever found was a metre wide, hanging off a tree as huge as a heron's wingspan. We also have the smallest maple leaves in Canada. You hardly notice the Douglas Maples all year until now, when they turn scarlet and leap right out of the bush at you. When you get the two together you have perfection. That is why we are having a party here — a maple party. It is a quaint west coast custom.

"If you stay here a while you'll get to love them. Did you know that this month was called 'time of the changing of the colours of the leaves' in one of the Salish languages? Our maples are subtle here in their changes. Easterners say that our maples can't hold a candle to theirs but I'm not so sure. Although I bet they have maple parties too. It is probably a quaint trans-Canadian custom.

"And the leaves are so useful. You can leap in them, use the stems to whip up Soopalallie-berry ice cream and steam a fish in

them. You can even stick them on a flag and wave them. In November of 1964, Canadians proposed the maple leaf flag for the first time. We debated over including the *fleur-de-lis* and Union Jack but in the end, a simple autumnal leaf seemed just right. They flutter down around every Canadian from the Pacific to the Atlantic regardless of religion, language, cultural origin and politics. And then they quietly rot into the earth.

"In fact, what leaves are best designed for is decomposing — tons of organic matter creeps slowly into the earth via an army of bacteria and minibeasties. Then next spring, there will be a rich layer of humus cloaked with a delicate lace shawl of skeleton leaves that will fly up into the air with the equinoctial gales. Speaking of gales, November was called, by that same Salish nation, 'month of the shaking of the leaves.' It's a signal that the golden time is over ...."

I wouldn't be able to trust myself to go further. It is an emotional subject, these leaves. I am sort of attached to the ideas of Canada and rich soil and tranquillity and having golden piles of leaves to leap into. Next party I go to, I'll just stick to the weather.

FUNGUS AMONG US:
SHERLOCK HOLMES AND THE MUSHROOM MYSTERY

The rain had ceased at last and a sickly autumn sun shone upon a land which was soaked and sodden with water. Wet and rotten leaves reeked and festered under the foul haze which rose from the woods. The fields were spotted with monstrous fungi of a size and colour never matched before — scarlet and mauve and liver and black. It was as though the sick earth had burst forth into foul pustules; mildew and lichen mottled the walls, and with that filthy crop, Death sprang also from the water soaked earth.

So wrote Sir Arthur Conan Doyle, in *Sir Nigel*, 1906. He was the guy who created Sherlock Holmes. But, mark my words, when the historians are analyzing the milestones of the millennium, what he will really be remembered for is launching a civil war between the Kingdom of Britain and the honourable Kingdom of Fungi — a war which has spread and festered throughout the world. It is not mushrooms that are foul pustules, but his words about these magnificent fungi.

Mr. Doyle (he should never have been knighted) was alliterative and convincing but he was wrong. The autumn sun is not sickly; it is simply an autumn sun. Leaves do not fester; they decompose. The haze that rises from the woods is not foul; it is pungent. Fungi are not monstrous and the earth is not sick with foul pustules; he must have been blind and dull witted. If he had actually spent any time at all in the woods, he might have noticed that in fact, fungi are a sign of forest health. The earth, Mr. Doyle, is sick without them.

"Sir" Charles Baudelaire (he should have been the one knighted) knew intuitively the importance of fungi when he wrote his poem "Intimate Associations," 50 years ahead of Mr. Doyle's diatribe.

> The natural world is a spiritual house, where the pillars,
> that are alive, let slip at times some strangely garbled words;
> Man walks there through forests of physical things that
> are also spiritual things,
> that watch him with affectionate looks. As the echoes of
> great bells coming from a long way off
> become entangled in a deep and profound association,
> a merging as huge as night, or as huge as clear light,
> odors and colours and sounds all mean — each other.
> Perfumes exist that are cool as the flesh of infants,
> fragile as oboes, green as open fields, and others exist also,
> corrupt, dense and triumphant,
> having the suggestions of infinite things,
> such as musk and amber, myrrh and incense,
> that describe the voyages of the body and soul.
> (From *News of the Universe*, translated by Robert Bly.)

Baudelaire was no mycologist but he had a profound understanding of the natural world. On the publication of his poems in 1857, he was fined and the book was banned as offensive to public morals. Which just goes to prove that those who control knighthoods and censorship should read up on fungi.

What Baudelaire knew was that the natural world is intimately associated in ways that he hadn't even begun to dream about. Fungi form one kingdom of organisms that has intimate associations with just about every plant and animal of the forest that ecologists care to turn an inquiring eye upon. Fungi are organisms that lack chlorophyll, so they have to rely on relationships with others. One such intimate relationship, called "mycorrhiza" (silent "h"), has been forged by fungi and plants through time. This is not a dysfunctional relationship. The fungus absorbs nutrients and water from the soil and sends them to its host plant. The plant in turn provides sugars from its own photosynthesis. To do this, the mushroom forms an under-

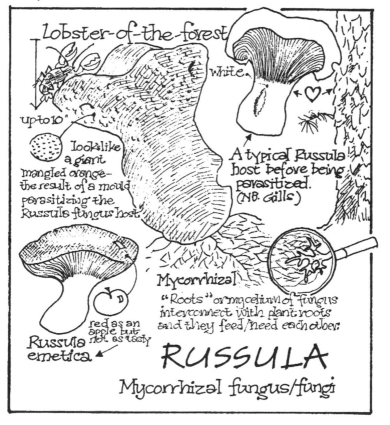

Lobster-of-the-forest

white.

up to 10"

Looks like a giant mangled orange- the result of a mould parasitizing the Russula fungus host

A typical Russula host before being parasitized. (NB. Gills)

Mycorrhizal

"Roots" or mycelium of fungus interconnect with plant roots and they feed/need each other.

Russula emetica

red as an apple but not as tasty

RUSSULA

Mycorrhizal fungus/fungi

ground network of little white filaments, called "mycelia," that thread through the earth. Mycelia attach onto the roots of the plant and they feed each other.

Probably three quarters of the world's plants have mycorrhizal associations. Spruce, Douglas-fir, hemlocks, pines, Garry Oak, alder and birch all rely on mycorrhiza fungi to deliver crucial nutrients. Far from being "foul pustules," the two kingdoms are joined "as huge as night." There are also saprophytic fungi, that Mr. Doyle would seize upon as evidence of "the filthy crop." But again, he should have listened to (Sir) Charles, that others exist corrupt (maybe) but "dense and triumphant." Without these fungi, we would have no mechanism for decay, no soil, no decomposing trees to house insects, voles, salamanders, red squirrels, pine martens, owls, woodpeckers — all watching "with affectionate looks."

Mycorrhizal and parasitic examples of fungi appear during this month. The soaked and sodden land of October gives rise to fungi of every colour of the rainbow. There are so many species of fungi that only a fraction have been recorded. The kingdom is so large that the thousands of mushrooms that you can see with the naked eye are just a few percent of the whole. Space doesn't allow me to mention them all, so I have selected my own particular eccentric favourite, *Hypomyces lactiflorum*, the Lobster-of-the-Forest, a parasitic mould that transforms the mushroom of a mycorrhizal fungus called *Russula* into a new form.

I recorded my last trip into the woods *à la* Doyle/Baudelaire:

The rain had ceased at last and a warm autumn sun shone upon a land which was soaked and rich with water. The forest was spotted with magnificent fungi of a size and colour never matched before — scarlet and mauve and orange and white. One enormous one halted us as it burst tumbling out of the earth. Its fleshy, dimpled, folded skin, the colour of a September sunset, reminded us of a newborn infant, fragile as an oboe, dense and triumphant, and having the suggestions of infinite things that describe the voyages of the body and soul.

November

SLUGS AT THE SPEED OF LIGHT:
LAND MOLLUSCS ON THE MOVE

Starlight might reach us at the speed of light but slugs are faster. Stars give us some clues about quantum mechanics but slugs have their own secrets for us to discover and they are much closer to study. This is my conclusion after spending some hours at the side of the road rescuing Banana Slugs and documenting their energy, mass and speed. Go to any coastal forest or even a suburban garden at this time of year and they are on the move to their winter quarters. They are easily identifiable; as our largest native land mollusc, they look like bananas with or without bruises. They sport "horns" and are often found heading in the direction of the nearest road to commit some kind of ritual mass suicide.

The metaphysics of slugs came to mind as I watched one of these creatures glide slowly but effortlessly over the uneven ground toward its destiny. I had read recently that matter is simply particles bonded by luck, and that mass is no longer measurable. Mass might be just the energy it takes to keep things from collapsing into nothing. The analogy of a wound-up clock weighing more than a unwound one struck me in particular. A slug is particles bonded with luck (and a bit of slime) that behaves like a slowly wound-up toy — its small apparent mass and amorphous form are defined by the energy propelling it across the tarmac to avoid the sun and an inevitable black hole (that's my earnest interpretation).

Physicists also say that surfaces and edges are really not what they appear to be; all particles are joined, but our perception makes things out to be separate. So an edge is simply a bunch of particles under a different kind of tension. To feel a Banana Slug is to grasp a glimmer of the truth of that thought. A Banana Slug does not really start or end. When you pick them up off the road to save them from annihilation, your hand gets covered in their viscous slime, which becomes a second skin. The particles in the slime are trying to fool you that the edge of your body is not really where you thought it was.

Just as I was debating whether to risk losing the edge of myself to that of a particular Banana Slug, a car came out of nowhere and bang! — the slug was gone. This vital, heaving creature disappeared in a metaphysical cloud of vapour and all that was left was a sheen of bad luck on the road. Judging from the lack of matter left on the road or on the tire, it was clear that the slug's previous form had been pushed out into space by its sheer life force — the luck bit. What else could have done it? Biologists will tell you it is the hydrostatic skeleton.

It was like the Big Bang in reverse. All the energy creating the slug's mass was released into the air in a moment and I could almost hear the proverbial alarm clock ringing. But it wasn't an alarm clock; it was the click click click of feet — six of them. Scurrying to the kill was a ground beetle with a great abdomen and scissor-like jaws extended. Beetles are unlike slugs in almost every regard but especially when it comes to drawing analogies from quantum mechanics. The beetle is the black hole into which matter is drawn. They are almost two dimensional in their denseness. Their legs and bodies are like imploding stars, so hard edged and black that you feel yourself drawn into them.

The beetle slid into what was left of the slug, jaws snapping, and dragged the particles of bad luck off the road within seconds. I looked down closely to watch his manoeuvres and noticed a little army of smaller insects rushing out from his

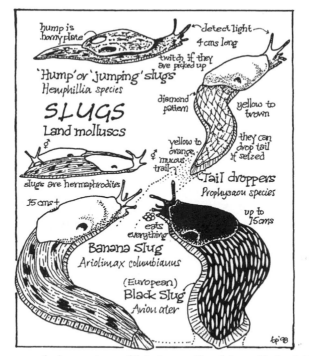

armpits toward the action of his jaws. Catching all the bits that fell from his jaws, these little mites had a great old feast. Now the other thing that I have heard physicists say is that they keep discovering smaller and smaller particles and that the tiniest particles don't act with any constancy. I decided that crawling all over the mites were tinier mites and crawling on them were tinier ones and so on, and who was to know if life still persisted in a form past the one-celled organism or not?

So entranced was I with this concept that I didn't notice the next passing motorist and wham! — all the beetles and the endless chain of mites were annihilated into the second dimension of the tarmac. At this stage, I began to wonder about our bizarre relationship with other forms of life. If we are all just a continuation of the same particles, separated only in our minds by a little bit of tension, why do we have such a cavalier attitude to our fellow particles?

At this stage a Northern Flicker moved onto the kill. It obviously loved squished ground beetles. Flickers are handsome birds that make you think of photons and the speed of light. They say photons are not always constant. The fact that photons can be slowed down and speeded up is what has caused us to rethink $E = mc^2$. When a flicker flies away with a universe of a Banana Slug, beetle and mite mingling with its particles, the speed of light increases. First you see a blinding flash of white as their rump feathers are exposed in flight. Then the atmosphere pulses in red or yellow as their wings rise and fall over the land. Sometimes the flashes are red, sometimes they are yellow, depending on if it is a red-shafted or yellow-shafted flicker and the different tensions of the bird's wing non-surface. Everywhere is charged with excited photons bouncing off this beautiful assembly of particles — a light so much faster than the dull light that oozed out of the slug or was swallowed up by the beetle's black surface.

But just when I thought I had cracked the essence of the speed of light, I watched a new slug attempt a crossing. It made for the shadow cast by a tree across the road and moved at the same rate as the shadow retreated. I realized that the slug was moving faster than the speed of light, and what was more, time had not stopped.

MARY POPPINS AND THE BIRD FEEDERS: SUPER FRAGILISTIC WINTER BIRDS

It is no accident that you won't find a reference to bird feeders in world literature until the landmark work of Mary Poppins. There is no mention of suet hanging outside the stable in Bethlehem. No ancient manuscript describes feeders under the eaves of Aztec temples and Genghis Khan did not suspend sunflower seeds in little net bags from his saddle. Chaucer describes how to fatten up doves for dinner but recreational bird feeders appear to be a modern concept. They didn't need feeders in those days: on the contrary, women and children scared them away from the bins from which the hard-earned grain was dispensed for growing crops, feeding animals or brewing whisky.

The relevance of this historical inquiry is to highlight some important considerations about bird feeders. Why did we start using them? Do birds need them? And what have we learned about feeding birds for pleasure since Mary Poppins?

Feeding birds for pleasure seems to have arisen concurrently with Victorian social reform and environmental havoc. The industrial revolution contributed habitat destruction, plate-glass windows and cat protection to its list of accomplishments, thereby wiping out large numbers of Europe's birds. The populace were alienated from the natural world and had to resort to flinging themselves into sidewalk paintings with flying ladies to connect to green places. They missed their cheeky little bird friends, so they set out some of their industrially acquired grain in the winter months to aid the survivors. The birds coming to the feeders were those that had had centuries to become supercalifragilisticexpealidocious opportunist eaters of grains lying around every farm homestead — they adapted. Feeding Little Robin

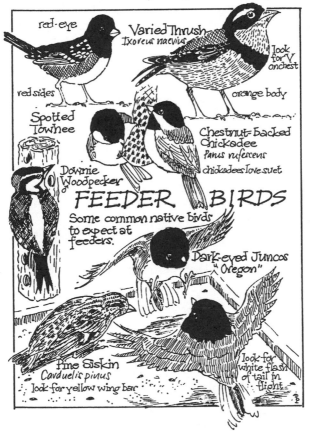

Redbreast became the symbol of urban Christian charity toward other forms of life. It was also a diversion from the more complicated problems of caring for needy humans.

Enter 20th-century west coast North America and we have the beginning of the dilemma. Do birds need feeders? Most of the above paragraph applies to the North American situation. We even brought over those cheeky little birds because we missed them, such as the House Sparrow, Rock Dove (or domestic pigeon — the one Chaucer liked to fatten up) and the European Starling. These birds had already won the Russian roulette of surviving the chimchimminies of the industrial revolution, displacing more timid species. So the answer is in part "no"; it would be preferable if women, children and any willing Mary Poppins were employed to scare them away. They are quickly displacing the entire world's bird populations.

Now comes the thrust of the dilemma — having wrought havoc on our native bird population, do we owe these species a bit of charitable spoon-full-of-sugar-helps-the-medicine-go-down assistance? Birds that were already on the coast, such as Chestnut-backed Chickadees, Dark-eyed Juncos, Spotted Towhees and Song Sparrows, had no experience with grain and suet available in dispensers, although they had been opportunists at human dwellings for millennia (a growing trend as their habitat was ripped out in favour of lawns and petunias). In colder weather, Pine Siskins, Northern Flickers, Red-breasted Nuthatches, House and Purple Finches, Brewer's Blackbirds and Varied Thrushes will also come and benefit from food supplies. So bird feeders can be a good idea if used judiciously to reduce winter die-off — birds that perish in bad weather because they have insufficient food to sustain them. But we have learned something about the subject since Mary Poppins.

The trouble with creating an artificial food supply for animals is that it can backfire on you. The feeder might attract native birds that normally wouldn't hang around and thereby upset the natural balance. The classic example of this is attracting jays who later will prey on songbird populations. It also follows that if you have created an artificial food supply and you inadvertently cut it off, some inadvertent culling will happen too.

The bird feed itself can been a problem in a variety of ways — a means of bringing weed species into areas and a distributor of salmonella and other bacterial infections. Finally, what bird feeders have done like nothing else before is provide a perfect hunting ground for cats. So here are some helpful suggestions to ease the dilemma.

Field Notes

1. Locate bird feeders so that there is cover for birds but not so close that they are vulnerable to cats. Put up a metal ring on the pole to prevent cats and rats. Better yet, keep cats indoors.

2. Mouldy seed can be fatal to birds. Because birds will spill feed on the ground where it gets mouldy, the feeder should be moved regularly.

3. As a rule of thumb, small millet grains and sunflower seeds are pretty safe and benefit our native birds the best. Never use popcorn and avoid cracked corn, unless you want to join Chaucer with a pigeon roast.

4. Discourage European Starlings; put your suet close under the bird table and put it in a container that the starlings cannot cling to very well, such as onion net bags.

5. Once started, don't abandon your dependents until you are sure a natural food supply is available, especially during bad weather.

6. The best thing you can do for birds is restore native shrubs in your backyard. It is worth a thousand feeders and will provide as much enjoyment. Then you can also skip points 1 to 5.

ESTUARIES: A PLEASANT WALK, A PLEASANT TALK

If you are in need of a stimulating conversation, I recommend bivalves — clams, oysters, mussels — as they are all refreshingly original in their views. Lewis Carroll, who wrote "The Walrus and The Carpenter," knew this.

> "O oysters, come and walk with us!"
> The Walrus did beseech.
> "A pleasant walk, a pleasant talk
> Along the briny beach."

Or better still, the coastal estuaries, the liveliest places along the coast in November. An estuary is where a river or creek runs into the sea. It is the meeting place of land, saltwater and freshwater, and like any place where different species from different habitats mingle, there is lots of chat.

The constants in a winter estuary are the flow of the freshwater and the changing of the tides. Listening to their dulcet tones soothes the mind after the drone of traffic. The mingling of salt- and freshwater gives rise to perfect conditions for billions of algae that range in size from the single-celled diatoms to 20-foot-long kelp. Algae is the food on which our ancestors have been feeding since the beginning of time so start your morning with a wave hello. As you look out over the seemingly calm bay, see if you can pick up snippets of news from the seething mass of competing bodies out there who continue to dine on algae. The minibeasts that devour diatoms alone are more numerous and cunning than any taxation system yet devised. Even on a cold November day, a Salish Sea estuary is a hotbed of activity.

PACIFIC HERRING
Clupea harengus pallasi
12"

herring spawn
18"
HARLEQUIN DUCK
"Thank-you swimmers, you Supernatural Ones"
First Nations grace

The abundance of these minibeasts is what draws all the other conversationalists. Bivalves comb the water and muse on international currents. Shore crabs glean breakfast from the rocks and are good listeners. Flocks of waterfowl and shorebirds fly in from the north to gossip over the winter. We have classy Harlequin ducks that don't talk much but stun you with their plumage. Wigeon lull you with their whistles. Flocks of little black-and-white Buffleheads buzz around you like tuxedoed waiters. Big black scoters ride the waves farther out while scaups, grebes and Oldsquaws try to get a word in over the loons. Mergansers puff out their head crests before pontificating.

I find eel-grass beds particularly good places in which to hang out with migrating shorebirds. There you are amongst the Dunlin, Sanderling and Spotted Sandpipers, sharing tips on the weather, snooping around the mud and making little peep noises when the mood seizes. If you go early enough in the morning, you can say hello to our charming *Mustelids*, the River Otter and Mink. Where else can you smell and be greeted warmly? Meanwhile, up in the shore trees left by thoughtful waterfront owners, Bald Eagles and Northwestern Crows are casually blethering away as they wait for errant Pink and Chum Salmon. Then as the tidewaters swirl back over your boots, the Cutthroat Trout move quickly into the beds while the Great Blue Heron follows behind — a shy but brilliant conversationalist.

Herons, mink, crabs; like the humble oyster, they give us pleasant walks and talks. So where do you go to these speakeasies? Anywhere the freshwater from the land is left to run uninterrupted to the sea, from the grand entrance of the Fraser to the ghostly remnants of culverted creeks with forgotten names. Sometimes they appear as mudflats and other times the estuary is simply marked by a small channel through the rocks and sand.

Named or not, these places are as threatened as good conversation because there are few forms of protection for them. This is a worry for anyone who enjoys the company of things that smell, scavenge and make peep noises in public. Part of the problem is that they lie in a jurisdictional no-man's-land. Migratory wildlife and oceans are in international jurisdiction;

rivers are local, unless they are navigable when they become, like non-migratory wildlife, provincial or state regulated; pollution in the water is regional; land use below the tide line is national, land use above the tide is local ... the tragedy is that people don't talk to one another when it comes to shoreline issues.

Things are looking up, though. Many have recognized that we need to get our act together and various shoreline stewardship initiatives are being supported widely. Getting to know these areas and having conversations with all concerned is a pretty good start. If we don't do something then we shall end up like the Walrus and the Carpenter.

> "O Oysters," said the Carpenter.
> "You've had a pleasant run!
> Shall we be trotting home again?"
> But answer came there none —
> And this was scarcely odd, because
> They'd eaten every one.

ANTLER ENVY: DOES AND STAGS WITH THE RACKS

Antler-tedium. It is the condition that some people fall into at the slightest mention of the word. I suffered from it for years; antlered animals were associated with a vast, tedious culture of checked shirts, pickup trucks and out-of-focus photos of large men grinning with their antler trophies. It was hard to get past the antlers to the animal within, as if they were fellow conspirators in the game. Come to think of it, it was hard to get past the checked shirts to recognize the animal within. But time has enabled a revisitation of these symbols and refashioned them in a new light.

It was the Irish Elk antlers in the bog that really made me stop and look at antlers in a new light. Irish bogs are well out of the context of checked shirts and bush. One is hard pressed to find a bush in the entire Irish countryside. The Irish Elk was an early ancestor of our elk, carrying a stack of antlers nearly four metres (11 feet) wide — heavier than the entire rest of its skeleton. It became extinct during the Pleistocene era, not surprisingly. The

Irish checked shirts either became extinct shortly afterwards or emigrated to Canada. One elk happened to fall into a bog and the antler has been preserved in all its splendour. Stroke it in your hand and you can see the grooves that formed when the veins were coursing with virile blood through the velvet. Even those most dedicated to antler-tedium cannot pass by this amazing testimony to male exuberance and not be impressed.

Since then, I have tried to look at antlers in the same way that I attend delicate wildflowers and newts, with the eye of an untrained sensualist. First of all, antlers are attached to a sensual animal. On the coast, we have the Columbian Blacktail Deer as our understated testimony to male exuberance. Blacktails are a small but stalwart coastal deer that is a subspecies of the larger Mule Deer of the interior. I mark the seasons by the dances of

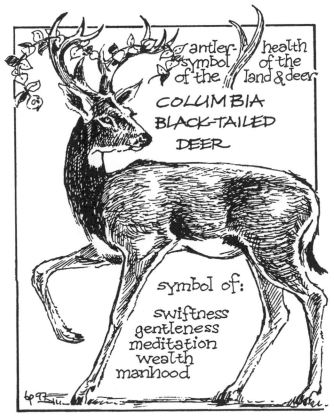

antler-symbol of the health of the land & deer

COLUMBIA BLACK-TAILED DEER

symbol of:

swiftness
gentleness
meditation
wealth
manhood

the bucks and the story of their antlers. In April, the horn buds appear with the Salmonberry buds. June-July, they grow their velvet — a lush, sensitive skin that coats the antlers like moss on rocks. August to October, the velvet falls off as the hormones rise, hardening the antler bone underneath. Alder saplings are rubbed raw, the red of the inner bark mingling with the blood of the velvet. The night air in the autumn rut is full of the clashes of the antlers. When December closes, it is the time of the casting-off of antlers.

So this month is the time to go and find discarded antlers and ponder them from some different angles. As you walk back through the forest, hold the antlers on your head and try to walk between the trees. This requires great skill and daring, and causes passers-by to quickly round up their children from possible attacks. Imagine why antlers evolved, when they patently slow down one's progress through the forest. The clue is to consider both the condition and number of prongs and food sources as you walk. I used to believe that the number of prongs was related to age and virility, but that is not exactly right — antlers are a reflection of the food sources and the mineral content of the soil more than age or hormones.

For a new perspective on antlers, imagine you are a doe looking for a mate that is holding good territory with ample food. You go for the laddie with the big rack. This realization has helped me to understand checked shirts a little bit better. All this time, I thought the biggest racks just advertised the virility of the bearer and not their shopping skills.

It must be said that despite their stalwart, courageous hearts and virility, many bucks around the Salish Sea have simple, single-pronged antlers which speak to us eloquently. It tells us that the soil is generally low in nutrients. We have occupied much of both their summer grazing and the winter shelter of old-growth forests with their windfall of tree lichens and sheltered, browse-filled openings. Allowing them to graze in our gardens is simply an act of remediation, but petunias do not make the beast. Men probably feel the same way. I am learning to look again at both antlers and checked shirts — with and without the velvet.

December

RAMPANT BUFFLEHEADS: NEW AGE HERALDRY

Everyone needs a coat of arms — a little heraldic crest that you sew on your winter coat when you go out to do battle with the wind, traffic and other fierce dragons. A coat of arms will give you a sense of security when other things seem to fail. It is a tried-and-true tradition. Ask a British or a First Nations historian; they'll tell you how important they are. For as long as either culture can remember, adorning themselves with their crests was a necessity for survival. Heraldic crests tell people who you are and where you come from. They represent your pledge of responsibility to the patch of land that you inhabit with your clan. Traditionally, when you wore the crest you had the support of your clan — that was your security. In return you had to respect your turf and its inhabitants. This custom gave rise to ages of chivalry. It could be a burden at times, but it also made for more courteous behaviour around traffic lights.

Technically, in both cultures a coat of arms must contain symbols that are geographical, distinctive and presented with balance, simplicity and boldness. You have to be able to recognize them instantly in a misty moor or forest. The animals or plants (called "devices") used in the crests were either mythical, to denote great power and status (thunderbirds on the coast and

155

griffins in England), or important to the clan in some way. In England they were sometimes a pun on the name (for example, a Lady Newton would have a newt on her crest). Crests would often allude to a place by what lived or grew there (say, the House of Rose or Hummingbird Clan). Over the thousand-odd years they have been documented on either side of the world, heraldic crests have appeared for individuals, families, clans or towns. They were used in peace and war, a flexible emblem changing with the society. For whatever purpose, they had to be

a diminuitive, dapper diving duck that winters in estuaries and protected bays, and breeds on the interior lakes

rampant buffleheads

Bucephala ædororet nos

Sidney-by-the-sea coat of arms

BUFFLEHEAD
Bucephala albeola

♂

♀

original and used with respect. To that end the profession of heraldic expert arose, to make sure that crests were not taken in vain, abused, disrespected or copied.

For a while the old standards were rocked a bit. Everyone in the Old World was getting on boats and trying to drag gardant (guarding) unicorns and rampant mermaids with them. Meanwhile, here in the New World, sea bears and two-headed serpents were getting short shrift from the new arrivals and were banned from winter coats, along with the potlatches. Crests designed for misty moors didn't work in misty forests. New communities popped up and acquired crests that broke all the rules of heraldry — they didn't tell us where we were or represent our pledge of responsibility to the new patch of land that we'd moved to. They were crests that weren't geographical or original. Probably because we had not consulted with the heraldic experts here.

But that's all changing, I hope. I know of two heraldic experts in British Columbia. Both grew up with grannies who had buttons all over their clothes. Both have met the queen, but one grew up in a tenement in south London and the other grew up on a reserve near Port Alberni. These guys know the rules and share a few jokes about dragons, thunderbirds and the queen. They both are interested in each other's craft and tradition. A blend of the two might be the future — heraldry experts who know where you are, where you have come from and where you are going.

This is the case of the coastal town of Sidney, BC, which has changed its coat of arms. Returning the unicorn and rose to their habitat in merry England, they have emblazoned rampant Buffleheads and Arbutus/Madrone onto the crest, while keeping the boat and a lighthouse as symbols of recent history. It took a long time and protracted debate for the citizens of Sidney to come to this decision. But now they are spending their winter evenings sewing their new crests onto their winter woollies like knights of old and parading down the street. The crests show their respect for two eras and two fine symbols of their community. The Buffleheads, diminutive, dashing, dapper, dancing diver ducks, graphically stunning in black and white, arrive every winter in the bays in Sidney and elsewhere in the Salish Sea. They spend their summers in the Cariboo nesting in aspen trees. You can see them in the winter skimming to a halt in the water, using gravity and friction like ballet partners in an elaborate *pas de deux*.

The second icon is the Arbutus or Madrone, providing us with year-long glimpses of sensuous limbs and leathery leaves along the shores. They are bearing loads of scarlet berries these days that plump up the winter birds. And so sensuous limb and skim provide all the requirements of heraldry. The two symbols embody the geographical place, distinctiveness, originality and a token of humility. Rampant Buffleheads don't strike fear into the hearts of visitors quite like lions.

I have great hopes for this new trend. Individuals, families, towns can all join in. Griffins and thunderbirds can fly around the west coast together. Individuals could have crests of what lives in their backyards, like Red Alder emblazoning the *Cadborosaurus*. Salish sea clans could have otters curled round a great carpet of shootingstars. Alongside European fictitious martlets, they could have murrelets flying — a symbol of sea, forest and great resourcefulness. The crest of British Columbia could have a Grizzly Bear lying down with the existing lion in a pact of mutual respect. The possibilities are endless. We could have our heraldic artists restored once again to a higher status as keepers of integrity.

I have something in mind for my own Garry Oak clan with a raven's quill for a pen. I'll stitch away this winter and make my coat of arms. It will help me reach peace with the dragons of development and cold December days.

ARBUTAGE: BERRY WEAPON FOR URBAN BLIGHT

A mild solution for winter blues and urban blight is at hand. I call it "arbutage" (casting Arbutus seed + sabotage; "madronage" if you are in the United States — Madrone + sabotage). It is the passive yet expansive gesture of throwing Arbutus seeds at everything that offends you in the hope that the object of offence will one day be obscured behind a veritable forest of Arbutus trees. There is a great amount of pleasure in this activity — it alleviates frustration, it is constructive and physical, it has long-term possibilities of beautifying the city and has the added attraction of being entirely incomprehensible to most perpetrators of blight so that you carry out this activity right under their noses. An afternoon of casting Arbutus seeds at malls is remarkably satisfying. This is the perfect time for collecting and preparing Arbutus seeds for germination and also for viewing the worst of urban blight.

The technique is simple and entails five steps. First, take yourself to a dry, coastal spot (with a good view) around the Salish Sea where Arbutus trees are still growing. These are

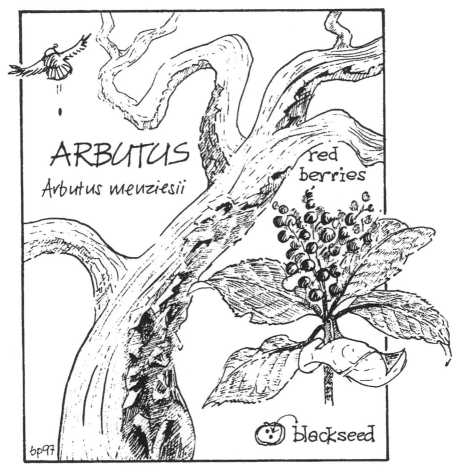

ARBUTUS
Arbutus menziesii

red berries

blackseed

bp97

supremely elegant trees, native to this region, that have broad leathery leaves which remain on the tree throughout the winter. Their trunks are mottled red and brown with peeling bark but smooth as babies' limbs. They have bright red berries which you cannot miss when the tree is producing. Not every tree produces so you might have to spend an entire morning wandering along a beach in between hot cappuccinos to find a berry-producing tree.

Step two, gather a bag full of the berries, keeping in mind that some should be left for the Cedar Waxwings and Band-tailed Pigeons which flock in great numbers to these trees. The berries are the richest oranges and reds and you might want to string a few together for an early Christmas garland. The Salish people used to make garlands of them for feasts. Take the remaining berries home and pour boiling water over them. Technically, you are simulating the passage of the berry through the intestines of a bird. I don't care to imagine what this experience would actually be like but boiling water certainly works to release the seed from the berry and activate its germination process.

The next step is to spend an hour or so over another cappuccino, separating the seeds from the berries and setting them on old newspapers to dry. You can scan the realtor adverts for the latest outcrops of urban blight and admire these little black seeds at the same time. They are tiny so place them carefully in an envelope or film cannister. You can sow them now or keep them in the refrigerator over winter.

For a good chance of germination, the areas where they are sown need to be relatively dry and exposed to full sunshine. Arbutus love rocky, thin, well-drained mineral soils. They sprout rapidly if they are left on sand and then neglected. Areas around chain-link fences, highway verges and cracks in cement are good places to start. I usually begin at the latest Arbutus Ridge/Madrone Crest-type subdivision in the hope that one day there will actually be an Arbutus once again gracing the shattered slopes of rock and cement.

I have attempted arbutage at rabid dogs, speeding cars and unkind people but the germination time of Arbutus doesn't approach 100 kilometres per hour. One is best sticking to inert objects of blight on the landscape.

Step four, the casting of the seeds, is simple enough. You select a pinch of seeds much like a pinch of salt and sprinkle them in these areas. The chances of rooting are quite high. I cast a hundred seeds last winter over a patch of bare earth and I had 60 seedlings by July. There is a bit of an attrition rate from grazing animals and the elements thereafter but I would put the odds that at least one or two out of a hundred will survive to adulthood if left alone. Even one tree is enough to soften the glare of the neon sign or the hard line of a cement wall.

For the less subversive, you can practise arbutage right in your own backyard, in your apartment block or outside your workplace. Wherever you put them, remember that the two things that Arbutus do not take kindly to are the lawnmower and the water sprinkler. As a follow-up exercise you can always strategically locate a little barricade of stones to protect the trees from these dual enemies. The most amazing areas of natural diversity in the region now are turning up in old dumps where weedeaters are noticeably absent.

Arbutus are the perfect tree for arbutage because they thrive in marginal areas so well. As a point of trivia, Arbutus are a member of the Heather family — a very tall member next to its smaller cousins of our native Salal, and the various rhododendrons and heather you find in rock gardens and *boutonnières*. If you have seen a heather species in action, you know that once they take root, they cling tenaciously to their spot and love a challenge. Alternatively, you can attempt some oaktage in dry areas, aldertage in gravelly areas or cottonwoodtage in wet places. Red Alder produce enormous numbers of seeds in the spring so you can commit endless aldertage.

You might get hooked on this form of silent, passive protest. As far as I know it is not possible yet to be imprisoned or fined for casting native seeds to the wind. I learned everything I know from a forester friend who hated the rigid sterility of tree plantations so he threw native tree seeds into the midst of the monocultures. It has the merits of other enjoyable activities — it could be construed as amoral as it requires a lot of climbing around silky smooth limbs and casting of wild seed. The progeny of wild Arbutus are worth it.

JOY TO THE NEW WORLD:
RUDOLPH THE RED-NOSED CARIBOU

It was once a great disappointment to me that I grew up in a place where there were no partridges in a pear tree. When I heard the chorus of "Joy to the World," the place where "heaven and nature sing" was somewhere between Bethlehem and the North Pole. European Reindeer were magic flying creatures and our Caribou were dull things that only migrated thousands of miles by foot. The west coast of North America was a seasonal wasteland where even our robin of the Thrush family couldn't compete with dainty namesake Robin Redbreast, nestled in the holly and the ivy of jolly olde Englande.

It has taken a while, but I think I am over it. Now I am faced with a member of the next generation looking at me with grave disappointment that we don't have Rudolophs, poinsettias or partridges in a pear tree outside. So this is my attempt to right the balance and add a regional magic to this seasonal backwater.

The first thing we did was put on our gumboots and go for an early morning walk in the rain in a sacred place where there are still ancient trees under which lowly beasts gather. We didn't have a comet burning overhead but the mist was rising off the sea below and there was a Ruffed Grouse in a fir tree. A flock of crossbills were working their way amongst the cones and the Pileated Woodpeckers were doing a Little-Drummer-Boy imitation. Juncos were scavenging on the ground for any discarded seeds. We inspected a log and disturbed a nest of Deer Mice who leaped away in fright. We came back to an estuary and I began to feel like a king (well, queen really) who was offering myrrh and frankincense to some little prince in his backyard. Out in the bay, we watched the Goldeneyes, Buffleheads and Pacific Loons. Slipping in and out of the water was a River Otter family. Orcas were breaching out by the herring balls. You get the idea: there seemed to be a festive carol brewing.

As we wandered along the shoreline, we ducked under Douglas-fir trees laden with cones, Arbutus trees heavy with scarlet berries, thickets full of white Snowberries, blood-red

Nootka Rose hips, dark green Salal and holly-like Oregon-grape. We were living in the midst of one giant Christmas decoration.

Thus inspired, we went home and have adapted a few of our Christmas traditions. Adapt is the operative word because old traditions die hard; I still have a soft spot for turtle doves, and some members of the family are quite attached to elves. The first thing we did was resist the desire to go out and deck the halls with boughs of holly. We planted copious amounts of Oregon-grape as our regional substitute. Instead of sending overbred, hothouse poinsettias to ageing aunts we created wonderful bouquets of Salal, Snowberries and Nootka Rose, twined up in Orange Honeysuckle. The Douglas-fir Tannenbaum this year has white-footed Deer Mice made out of cones and garlands of Arbutus berries hanging from it.

We are working on a manger scene of the estuary, making things out of *papier maché*, glue and poster paint. The food chain of loons, fish, mudshrimp and algae provides a far easier model for discussing the concept of death and rebirth than bearded men flying up into the sky. It also avoids the problem of trying to make the camels stand up properly. Cards and wrapping paper are a cinch now too. A block print of a Roughskin Newt with a bow, or a Dark-eyed Junco on a Snowberry, makes a stunningly original card.

Finally, we had fun rewriting some of the Christmas carols. "Deck the halls with boughs of Oregon-grape" and "Rudolph the red-nosed Caribou" didn't really take off but it was funny to a six year old. We did a revision of "The Holly and the Ivy" and added some comments about Scotch Broom, too. We tried some variations on "Dashing through the Salal" for an alternative "Jingle Bells," but had the greatest success with the "Twelve Days of Christmas." This might even make it into a new family tradition, despite some male members not wishing to appear too politically correct. To make a long story short, the last verse goes:

> On the twelfth day of Christmas, my true love sent to me, twelve woodpeckers drumming, eleven otters sliding, ten Deer Mice leaping, nine eagles waiting, eight whales a-breaching, seven wigeon swimming, six crossbills laying, five Goldeneye, four Dark-eyed Juncos, three Pacific Loons, two Buffleheads and a Ruffed Grouse in a fir tree.

HALCYON DAYS: CHATTER DARTS AT WINTER SOLSTICE

It should be a calm kingfisher day as you read this. The seven days before and seven days after the winter solstice are halcyon days — the ancient Greek days of peacefulness when the seas are calm and the Belted Kingfisher (*Ceryle alcyon*) has its time. Alcyon was the daughter of the wind god Aeolus. Her husband was drowned by the wild storms of the sea and so she threw herself into the sea to follow him. The gods rewarded such love and turned her into a kingfisher. Aeolus calmed the winds during the winter solstice to allow his daughter to lay eggs and raise her young. I discovered this story by accident, just like you discover a kingfisher — a flash of light followed by a chatter and splash.

The day I set out to write this article, it was calm for the first time in months, thanks to Aeolus. His earlier efforts at wind had been spectacular, with three months of incessant winter storms. I had walked toward the sea in the early morning to celebrate the winter solstice. It was perfection that day; some other god had inspired the Snowberries and Arbutus berries to shine and Alcyon was on her branch above a still sea.

There are probably only a handful of people who go through life on the coast failing to notice the kingfishers. These are the

BELTED KINGFISHER
Ceryle alcyon

flight arc

orange belt

no belt

♀

① 'Halcyon'
② 'Chatterdart'
③ 'Belted Queenfisher'
♂

bp98

birds that children learn first and old people forget last. On a still winter day, you can hear a kingfisher laugh from clear across a bay. You can hear them over the ferry horns. They look like Elvis Presley with his hair dishevelled after a good rock and roll in his blue suede shoes. They hover and plummet and splash and don't give a toss about you laughing with them.

The fine thing about kingfishers is that they ebb and flow with the storms. They retreat during storms to fish some quieter swamps but they return to the sea on these calm days. Maybe that's why the Greeks imagined that they might want to rear young in the winter; as good a time as any when you are relying on fish. In truth, the kingfishers here aren't laying eggs right now but they are courting, and in my mind, courting is far more halcyon than laying the eggs and rearing the young. A wild winter southeasterly describes child rearing better than a still sea.

I watched kingfisher courtship that morning. Although they both have blue breastbands, the female also has an orange band below — which is what I would describe as the belt. I think perhaps we should call them "belted queenfishers" since the king doesn't have a belt. Then again we could call them both "brassiered kingfishers" as this is technically what the blue bands look like on both sexes. Other names that have been put foward include "chatter darts" for their propensity to chatter before they plunge in at great speed (which also describes male courting behaviour adequately in most species).

Having to return to my own little chatter darts to get them off for school rituals involving Caribou and invasive holly species, I left behind the halcyon scene, climbed back up the hill and started my work day. I was so inspired by the kingfishers that I reached for my dictionary on symbolic and mythological animals and looked under "K". "K" is full of strange Australian creatures. But there, nestled between the Australian kestrel and kookaburra, was a kingfisher with an entire page of its own — a family of birds revered around the world for its symbolism of calmness during the solstice. I let out a chatter and darted for my computer. I checked the date and plunged into the story, blessing Aeolus that he had spared my own brassiered kingfisher on his crossings of the stormy seas and given us these halcyon days.

RATTLE OF RAVENS: WINTER RELIEF

Someone asked me what things I liked best about the winter on the coast. I told them the Salvation Army and Common Ravens. I admire them because when it comes to the darkest days of the year, I need something to shine a candle to. The common and endearing feature of these two is that they both rattle things and stay put at a time when everything else flies south. The Salvation Army is always here — at the street corners, rattling their bells. And ravens are always here — in the treetops, rattling their throats. It is just nice to know that there are some constants in life when nothing much else is.

If anything is constant it is ravens. They are constantly noisy and don't budge from their territory except when ungenerous human beings remove their roosts or worse, remove them. Left to their own devices, they'll cheer you up in the bleak midwinter with their friendly "kroks" and drive you nuts in the spring when the babies are let loose to the sky. You'll empathize with them in the summer when they hang out in the cool of an old fir, skulking from the tourists, until the Indian summer and a good moult gives them back their freedom. Every year it is the same old story and nothing pleases me more.

Loving ravens must be a sign of age or the times. I used to identify with birds like those Arctic Terns that raced around the planet. It sort of went hand in hand with admiring Simone de Beauvoir and existential crises. The rites of passage have occurred and my emancipation now lies in admiring the qualities of ravens. For instance, ravens are very cooperative. They are also into equal parenting. I have watched a male raven tenderly chew a piece of rotting crab and soften it with rain water to take back to its young. Having fed the ravenous offspring (yes, that is where the word comes from) the male stands by and guards the nest while the female goes out for a joy flight.

Playfulness is another admirable quality in a raven. Ravens play a great deal with each other, especially in flight. They grasp talons and shake in the sky. They do quick, 180-degree flips and dive-bomb objects of loathing like birds of prey. I have often felt like doing a 180-degree flip in committee meetings and frequently wish to dive-bomb objects of loathing but protocol compels me to remain upright and stationary.

Somehow they balance to perfection the dual roles of fool and king. If ravens feel the need to be assertive, they have little feathers above the eye which they can raise to make them look imperious. Also, the feathers on their legs can be fluffed out to give them a little substance. If you have failed in the realm of power dressing, try this technique of raising your eyebrows in annoying situations. I have yet to master the art of raising the hairs on my legs; there are too many of them.

Ravens' command of their realm is undeniable. As they fly over you, watch their eyes roving around. They are the world's opportunists; never a trick is missed. I have a rock upon which I periodically place scavengings — bits of carcasses from neighbouring farms — to lure ravens and sketch them. Usually within an hour, old raven has honed in on the spot and called the rest of the family over. They squabble over the meal, then flap off — great volumes of air accompanying their departure. They are a talented bunch at securing and hiding food and storing it for the lean times.

Raven admiration is not new. They have been admired almost unanimously across their entire realm which stretches round the northern hemisphere. The Raven Clan up in Haida Gwaii have composed stories that recognize the sterling virtues of humour, dignity, rampant opportunism and loyalty. The Vikings so admired these birds that they were deemed the messengers of the gods. Warriors adorned all their boats with them. So did the Celts and other pagans of the north. The only group that has not pledged allegiance to this chief of the crows is the English. The English have never liked ravens; to them they are a symbol of death and misfortune. They go so far as to use the collective noun — a murder of ravens. This is because in every place they tried to conquer, the natives were running around with raven symbols on their boats, uttering oaths in some indecipherable language.

Unfortunately, there are still some who can't sit comfortably with a raven within two kilometres for fear that the sky will fall on them or they will get their eyes pecked out. Hitchcock's

Northwestern Crow
Corvus caurinus

wedge-
shaped
tail of
raven

straight tail

RAVEN & CROW

shaggy
throat feathers

Common Raven
Corvus corax

movies have something to do with it. Apart from raiding the odd nest, ravens' habits are exemplary. They clean up the country-side of carrion, errant rodents, ailing animals and molluscs. When the young crows have hatched, ravens move in to control crow populations. The most atmospheric place to see ravens is in the heart of the rainforest. In cities, ravens have established some niches. They can be found near dumps and where there are crows breeding. You'll also find them near farms with livestock and by the sea. Keep an eye and an ear open as you walk along a shoreline this winter. If you have ravens nesting in your backyard, raise your eyebrows.

Ravens are easy to distinguish from their smaller black cousin, the Northwestern Crow, by their size if you see them together. You might pass a raven sitting alone in a tree and think, just another crow. But if you hear the noise of a champagne bottle popping or the rattle of an ancient drum, look up and catch the steely eye of a raven. She will be watching you and will respond favourably to a small conversation of "kroks" and "pruks." This generally alarms passers-by but I respond to them with my eyebrow trick. Ravens are nearly as big as eagles and bigger than our largest hawk, the Red-tailed Hawk. They have a great shaggy throat and powerful beak and are more solitary than the gregarious crows, though you might see a group of them at a carcass on a beach. They also have a longer, more wedge-shaped tail than a crow.

Despite the companionship which these birds offer, the raven is vulnerable. They are easy to victimize because they are such creatures of habit and territory. In Europe, where gamekeepers have persecuted them in the past, the raven has retreated to the few inaccessible patches of wildness left. That scenario is only too possible here. Their habitat is shrinking and so is the pagan memory. In many parts of northern Europe, they are a symbol of vanished wilderness. I hope that day doesn't come to the west coast. I need the raven to cheer me up in the middle of the winter, to keep me loyal to my place and my friends, let me not worry about my hairy legs and occasionally play the fool.

Further Reading

GENERAL NATURAL HISTORY

Cannings, R. and S. 1996. *British Columbia: A Natural History.* Vancouver: Greystone Books. A new classic. Look for the smaller companion series too.

Kirk, R. 1992. *The Olympic Rain Forest: An Ecological Web.* Seattle: University of Washington Press.

Kozloff, E.N. 1991. *Plants and Animals of the Pacific Northwest.* Seattle: University of Washington Press. A classic all-round guide.

Maser, C. 1989. *Forest Primeval: The Natural History of an Ancient Forest.* San Francisco: Sierra Club.

Royal British Columbia Museum Handbook Series. A great series of inexpensive handbooks covering a variety of different animal and plant groups in British Columbia. Some are out of print and only available in libraries. Many have been reprinted by UBC Press.

Stewart, H. 1998. *On Island Time.* Vancouver: Douglas & McIntyre.

Weston, J. and D. Stirling. 1986. *The Naturalist's Guide to the Victoria Region.* Victoria: Victoria Natural History Society.

GEOLOGY AND GLACIATION

Ludvigsen R. and Graham Beard. 1994. *West Coast Fossils.* Vancouver: Whitecap Books.

Pielou, E.C. 1991. *After the Ice Age: The Return of the Life to Glaciated North America.* Chicago: University of Chicago Press.

Yorath, C.J. 1990. *Where Terranes Collide.* Victoria: Orca Book Publishers.

Yorath C.J. and H.W. Nasmith, 1995. *The Geology of Southern Vancouver Island.* Victoria: Orca Book Publishers.

PLANTS, LICHENS AND FUNGI

Aurora, D. 1986. *All That the Rain Promises and More.* Berkeley: Ten Speed Press. About mushrooms.

Goward, T. 1994. *The Lichens of British Columbia.* Victoria: BC Ministry of Forests. Several slim volumes.

Lyons, C.P. and W. Merilees. 1995. *Trees, Shrubs and Flowers to Know in British Columbia and Washington.* Vancouver: Lone Pine Publishers. Excellent beginner's guide and lovely drawings of men in big hats for scale.

Parish, R. and S.M. Thompson. 1994. *The Tree Book: Learning to Recognize Trees in British Columbia.* Victoria: BC Ministry of Forests and Canadian Forest Service.

Pojar, J. and A. MacKinnon, eds. 1994. *Plants of Coastal British Columbia* (also entitled *Plants of the Pacific Northwest*). Vancouver: Lone Pine Publishers. The Bible for general plant identification.

Underhill, T.E. *Guide to Berries of the Pacific Northwest.* Vancouver: Hancock House.

MARINE LIFE

Ford, J. K.B., G. M. Ellis and K. C. Balcomb. 1994. *Killer Whales.* Vancouver: UBC Press, Seattle: University of Washington Press.

Harbo, R. 1999. *From Whelks to Whales.* Madeira Park, BC: Harbour Publishing.

Kozloff, E.N. 1987. *Marine Invertebrates of the Pacific Northwest.* Seattle: University of Washington Press.

Lamb, A. and Phil Edgell. 1996. *Coastal Fishes of the Pacific Northwest.* Madeira Park, BC: Harbour Publishing.

Ricketts, E., J. Calvin and J.W. Hedgpeth. Many editions. *Between Pacific Tides.* Stanford: Stanford University Press. Classic of the century.

LAND ANIMALS

Boror, D.J. and R.E. White. 1970. *Insects.* Peterson Field Guide
Series. Boston: Houghton & Mifflin.

Butler, R. 1997. *Great Blue Heron.* Vancouver: UBC Press.

Corkran C.C. and C. Thoms, eds. 1996. *Amphibians of Oregon,
Washington and British Columbia.* Vancouver: Lone Pine
Publishers.

Mason, A. 1999. *The Nature of Spiders: Consummate Killers.*
Vancouver: Greystone Books.

Peterson, R.T. 1990. *A Field Guide to Western Birds.* Boston:
Houghton & Mifflin.

Royal British Columbia Museum Handbook Series on mammals.
Six handbooks including: *The Rodents of B.C., The Insectivores of
B.C., The Bats of B.C., The Carnivores of B.C., The Hoofed
Animals of B.C.*

FIRST NATIONS

Carlson, K.T. 1997. *You are asked to witness: the Stó:lo in Canada's
Pacific Coast History.* Vancouver: Stó:lo Heritage Trust.

Elliott, D., Sr. and Janet Poth, eds. 1990. *Saltwater People.*
Victoria: Native Education School District 63 (Saanich).

Maud, R. 1978. *The Salish People: The Local Contribution of Charles
Hill-Tout.* Vancouver: Talonbooks.

Stewart, H. 1996. *Stone, Bone, Antler and Shell: Artifacts of the
Northwest Coast.* Vancouver: Douglas & McIntyre.

Turner, N. 1995. *Food Plants of Coastal First People.* Royal British
Columbia Museum Handbook. Vancouver: UBC Press.

Turner, D.B., ed. 1992. *When the Rains Came and Other Legends of
the Salish People.* Victoria: Orca Book Publishers.

U'mista Cultural Society and B. Compton. 1998. *The Living
World: Plants and Animals of the Kwakwaka'wakw.* Alert Bay:
U'mista Cultural Society.

POETRY, MYTHOLOGY AND CULTURAL ATTITUDES TO NATURE

Bly, R. 1980. *News of the Universe: Poems of the Twofold
Consciousness.* San Francisco: Sierra Club.

Cooper, J.C. 1992. *Dictionary of Symbolic and Mythological Animals.*
London: Thorsons.

Douglas, G. 1992. *Seascape with Figures: Poems Selected and New.* Victoria: Sono Nis Press.
Quammen, D. 1988. *The Flight of the Iguana.* New York: Delacorte Press.
Thomas, K. 1983. *Man and the Natural World.* London: Penguin Books.

HISTORY
Hayman, J., ed. 1989. *Robert Brown and the Vancouver Island Exploring Expedition.* Vancouver: UBC Press.
Mackie, R.S. 1995. *The Wilderness Profound: Victorian Life on the Gulf of Georgia.* Victoria: Sono Nis Press.

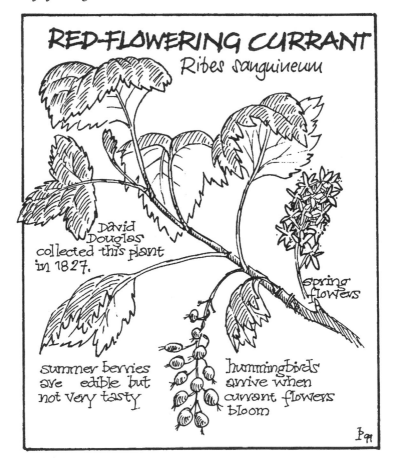

Index

Briony Penn is a young woman of great energy and many talents. She travels BC extensively: sailing as a naturalist aboard yachts giving ecotours along the coast; visiting projects for The Land Conservancy, of which she is a director; conducting workshops in bioregional mapping and environmental education; and this winter, she found time to ride, unclothed, down Vancouver streets as Lady Godiva. She and her husband design interpretive facilities such as the Gwaii Hanas Visitor Centre on the Queen Charlotte Islands. Briony has also taught Environmental Studies, Geography and the Restoration of Natural Systems as a sessional lecturer at the University of Victoria. She is a frequent speaker at conferences and symposia across North America.

"I have just finished reading *A Year on the Wild Side* from cover to cover and it is terrific. Congratulations!"
—Robert Bateman, wildlife artist

"Penn also has the knack of finding beauty in unlikely places. She deftly melds fable and fact."
—Anne Moon, *Times Colonist*, Victoria

"Relevant, timely, engaging, practical, instructive and memorable. [In her] lively, chatty style, Penn bases her commentaries on a solid foundation of research, observation and personal experience."
—Nancy Turner, *BC Studies*

"Briony Penn — wild girl, naturalist, ecosystem mapper, columnist and activist — is just about the only person alive who makes me think my brain isn't destined to be a wholly owned subsidiary of Time-Warner, CBS and Disney."
—Elizabeth Nickson, *The Globe and Mail*